Poems

from

A Smorgasbord

Mind

Poems

From a Smorgasbord Mind

D. B. Clark

Contents

Love is Defined
As Nearly Devine or Out of Your Mind

In the Final Draft

Introduction

Many poets, old and modern, seem to specialize in a limited number of forms and kinds of content. They employ these few styles to express their thoughts and feelings about only a few subjects, and then their reputations rest upon the best of these poems. Perhaps their notable poems are the result of their years of practicing similar poems, over and over again, until they are truly worthy. Thus, they might have said significant things to say about, grief or death, and they have said these things very well.

For me, reading such poets may be at first meaningful and pleasurable, but then eventually boring. Of course, I may be the only one who has this problem, but I hope that by varying my styles, and more importantly, my subject matter, I will avoid boring other readers who have a similar problem. I find it easy to do this because I enjoy writing about anything that strikes me as unusual. Since I have a rather idiosyncratic slant on life, that's just about everything.

I call this peculiar personal trait:

My Smorgasbord Mind

I have a smorgasbord mind,
My brain seldom dines on any one thing.
I can snack on thoughts of most every kind,
On whatever exotic thoughts the server may bring.

It's a wonder all the thoughts that I find
Can nourish my excessively overactive brain,
But the variety of thoughts in my smorgasbord mind
Are what's keeping me alive, and more or less sane.

So, be my guest, and dine at my table. I hope that you enjoy eating the smorgasbord poetic meal I've prepared for you, as much I enjoyed preparing the meal.

Weep or Smile,
Everyone's a Child Once in a While

I suspect that, as I, you have experienced what may be the typical course of conversation at a dinner party. The guests break the ice by talking about what most people have in common and what is the least controversial—the family— recent family events, amusing or not so amusing relatives, and even sadness at the inevitable loss of loved ones. But perhaps most of the talk centers around the children—their cuteness and of course their brilliance. It could be that part of our fascination with our children comes from our longing for the part of ourselves that wants to return to the innocents of childhood, when fairies and other fantasies were more pleasurable than the painful reality of growing up.

As the appetizers are sampled, along with a little wine, the guests become more relaxed, realizing through this mutual sharing that they are more alike than different. The poems of the beginning of our evening together reflect upon and celebrate this mutuality.

Rest in My Lap

My lap of love now holds my hurting child
And warms away the wounds that life may bring.
The arms of love's embrace are opening.
The lips of love have gently kissed and smiled.

And with these gifts of love I'll ease your pain,
And you will leave my lap and challenge life,
Then grow so strong you'll master every strife
So you won't need my gifts of love again.

But when in time my loving strength has gone,
My lap, my arms, my lips have had their day,
I will not ask, but I won't turn away
If you should offer me a lap to rest upon.

Who is the parent and who's the hurting child?
In time, we may be both if love has smiled.

New Baby Shower Song

Now that you're married and having a baby,
Forget about certainty, *your life's about maybe.*
But that is alright, when it's over and done
You'll have a sweet daughter or a handsome son,
And after the she, or the he's, gone away
Then a little more certainty may come back your way.

Neighbors

Neighbors gather all outdoors,
Wondering what the other folks are doing.
Oh, they gossip, and that's okay,
That is just the folksie way
Of finding out what's old and new in
Neighborhoods.

So let's let every couple have its say,
Then when they go back home at night,
To finish up the evening chores,
'Cause that's the way its meant to go
Where all the people know
What all the people know
In neighborhoods.

Swinging

Swinging, swinging, and my feet reach up to the sky,
Then suddenly a delightful drop, and the earth is passing by.
With a mighty pump, then my happy rump
Again is mounting high.
Then I plunge back down, almost touching ground—
So happy I could cry.

Swinging, swinging, not caring you think I'm insane,
It feels too good to complain.
Singing, singing, I am singing this song while swinging,
Over and over again.

I'd Love to Live in Fairy Land

I'd love to live in Fairy Land,
Where children play each day.
I'd romps with elves, and fly with sprits,
And chase the trolls away.

I'd fight with cringing giants,
And toss the cowards down,
Then drawn the magic sword
To win the kingly crown.

But now I'm reading all of this
To children on my knee,
And you know what I see?
That child who romps in Fairy Land,
That happy child is me.

The Fairy Swing

Let's go down to the Fairy Garden,
There's a swing there we can ride to the sky.
And when we reach the swing's highest moment,
The joys we seek will then multiply.
For that's when we'll be where the fairies have gone
Where night is a dream and it's always dawn.
So let's go to the Fairy Garden
And set ourselves in the swing,
And this time, let's swing even higher
To see what *more* our swinging can bring.

Why's Cassandra Sad?
Polly's No So Bad.

Goody Goody Two Shoes
Pollyanna sings no blues.
Instead, you be Cassandra,
Foretelling blackest night,
But if you claim that all is wrong
Then life is never right.

So I will wear my pretty shoes
And never sing the blues.
And you can be Cassandra
And fill your life with bile.
And I will face the future
With Pollyanna's smile.

January 14th
Valentines Day

Valentine day's a whole month away,
But I write this ditty to honor that day.
We cling together when each has a need
For hearts that are loving also can bleed.
Though it's not romantic to allude to our pain,
On this day of passion and sunshine not rain,
But hearts that are caring are ones that speak true—
I don't love an angel, I only love you.
So this is my pleasure, and this is my way
To show that I love you on "Valentines" day.

The Dimensions of Movies

My grandson was considering the dimensions of movies.
The three-D movie had captured his thought.
What were the director's intensions,
What mood by this technique would be caught?

Was it fear from the out-thrusting objects,
Or awe at those spiraling lights,
Or disgust from the splattering gore,
Exploding from fist-pounding fights?

And could there be *higher*-D movies?
Like forth, fifth, or sixth, or more?
Would that mean adding taste, smell and texture
To all of that wild flinging gore?

Then finally we got back to basics,
Two-dimensional pictures were there from the start,
But the director also needed great stories
To capture the audience's heart.

And then I proposed a new question,
How would *one*-dimension movie start?
He didn't have a ready and smart answer,
But I had my own—though just in part.

In physics, one dimension is a dot
That doesn't exist in space
And *that* is the kind of movie
That currently too often takes place,

Continued . . .

Movies that are empty of meaning,
Action that takes you nowhere,
Thoughts that have no true purpose,
People who don't seem to care.
That's why, considering such movies,
Let's not even bother to look,
That's why I'm glad that my grandson
Reopened a *one-dimensional* book.

Another Lonely Elf

Know thyself, my lonely elf.
You are just a porcelain piece,
So very small, you're not tall at all,
A tiny statuette that only lives on my shelf.

So why are you so very dear to me?
Because, when I take time to know myself,
I see myself in thee.
Because, although *I* may be tall,
I sometimes think I'm nothing much at all—

Especially when all my loved ones fail to call.
Then I am just another lonely elf upon my shelf—
Of all the elves, the loneliest of all.

On the Steps of Time

My wife had varnished the stair steeps
With a lustrous Danish oil,
And though we waited all day,
With the sun overhead at a broil
The stair steps would never dry,
And it seems they still will be wet
Even after *we* both dry up and die.

So I guess I will end this sad rhyme
With a truth that is almost sublime,
Since we both left a trace, on the still-wet staircase,
We may have left footprints
On the proverbial stair steps of time.

Son, On Receiving Your License to Fly

All of your life you've been flying,
But just in your venturesome mind,
Sailing the vast realms of reason,
Leaving all of your classmates behind.

But now you're using an airplane
To reach where others have flown
And you're also authorized to carry me
So you'll no longer fly all alone.

But I wonder which flight is more risky.
As a pilot, leaving nothing to chance,
You limit your risk to what is unknown
Since each flight is planned in advance.

Continued . . .

But no flight plan is filed for the journey
Through that uncharted and vast mental zone,
Where one can encounter those terrors
One might wish one had never known.

But fly in your well-controlled airplane,
Even take me for a ride on the air,
Yet never fearing to fly in your mind—
For your father will always be there.

It is Not the House That's Important

It's not the house that's important,
But the people who live therein.
It is not the body that's important,
But the spirit inspiring men.

It's not the word that's important,
But the thought that struggles to rise.
It's not the fault that's important
But the truth that comes when one tries.

It's not the face that's important,
But the love that shines though the eyes.
It is not what's written that's important
But what learns in becoming wise.
And not even that learning is important—
What's important is what one learns when one dies.

My Big Sister

Big Sister, you're Mother, 'cause Mother's not here.
Big Sister, Big Sister, you've banish my fear.
Someday I'll leave you, I won't need you then.
Big Sister, don't worry, be sure that is when
I'll call you to thank you for all that you've been—
A mother who loved me when Mother was gone.
Big Sister, I promise your love will go on.
When I am a mother as caring as you,
My child will love us as a loved child should do—
As now I most certainly have great love from you.

A Reason to Continue Trying.

This heavy old blanket is comforting.
It keeps the heat upon my shoulder,
And I can face what this night may bring,
And even contemplate growing older.

Yet in the night, the past still calls to me
And asks if it is time for dying.
Is this the end that I was meant to see,
And if that's so, why should I continue trying?

And then another warmth flows over me,
I hear a voice beneath the blanket, sighing,
And in the darkness, I again can see,
Another reason to delay my dying.

She is not old enough to come with me.
To leave her now would leave her crying.
To wipe away those tears will always be
A reason to continue trying.

Pleasing Others

Pleasing him, pleasing her, pleasing them,
This is more than just a noble martyr's whim.
This *is* the very reason I'm alive.
This is the reason that I strive,
This is what there *is* and all there'll ever be,
'Cause all this pleasing others pleases me.

I Had to be Late

Sorry I'm late. I had to baby-sit for my best friend's four-year
old child.
Brave little Kathy, we played, and she smiled,
And yet, I sensed she had fears—
Although no one had yet told her that mother had just died.
She was taking her nap, when her father returned,
And I continued holding back my tears
To crush my friend to my chest
When the man broke down and cried.
What else could I do but be with, and there, for him
And somehow see them through,
For isn't that what parents, and even best friends,
Always, *yes always,* must do.

A Double Life

When I was young, I knew my parents cared for me,
But still I often felt alone.
I didn't mind, it gave me time to know myself.
I did this "knowing" on my own.

There was a time, however, when my father died,
When loneliness is what I'd feel,
But that was not the same. Yes, I learned of fear,
But *emptiness* was now more real.

In adolescence, what I felt was strange and new,
An urge so strong it drove me wild.
For there was no one more important than the one
Who merely looked at me and smiled.

But gonad-driven lust was soon to lose its grip,
Since through its force I chose
A partner who would be as one with me,
Until our time as one would close.

But even we, though much in love, would drift apart,
Different edges, rubbing, often grind,
But then, at last, there came the perfect one
I never knew that I would find.

A child was born, a son who filled the void,
An emptiness I only guessed I had.
Yes, he would grow and go his separate way,
But even this would make me glad.

For he was such a perfect part of me
That I became much more than I had been.
When he was born, then I was born anew
My emptiness was gone again.

Continued . . .

We did together things I'd always done alone,
    Now, everything he did, I'd do,
And all the differences we had just built a bond
    Because we always talked them through.

And when at last that part of us that just is me
    Departs from us, there will be something new,
Where once a single life has been, a double life will be,
    For this is what we both had learned to do:

I will then leave him memories of things
    Together we had done
So he will know to banish all his loneliness,
    By bonding with another perfect son.

To Care Enough

I do what I can do so I will heal
    Before the tiny ills becomes too great.
That way I have at least some small control
    And know that age and death will have to wait.

But there are those, who make my life worthwhile,
    Who do not take the care I think they should,
So when I see that they are suffering,
    I wonder if the things I do are really good.

Would I still wish to live when they are gone?
    A life's that's long, and even one with health,
Without those loved ones living by my side,
    I'd be a dying pauper buried in my wealth.

Two Children Face Death

"Where have you been, Little Warrior?
You are swollen. Here's a scrape. There's a bruise.
Are you limping? There's a lump on your forehead.
Did you battle? Did you win? Did you lose?
Did comrades you trusted forsake you
Or, with valor, did they fall to the foe?
And who was that fiend that you battled?
Thought it scares me, I still have to know."

"My Father, you needn't have worried.
Though the foe was fearsome and foul,
I had learned when you toiled as my mentor
To face all my foes with a scowl
And spit in the eyes of those villains,

And show them my face not my fear.
And the comrades who fell died with pride.
And, Father, I didn't fight there alone.
You were always there at my side.

"So do not weep, Little Father,
I'm a man now, though my body's still small.
And, as one, we will face Death, together,
The next time he dares come to call."

Smarty Fox and Haughty Duck

A grinning duck was swimming down the stream,
Its wings tucked at its side.
I thought that I might hop aboard
And steal myself a ride.

The duck peered up the bank at me
To lift its head on high.
He flicked his beak and squawked aloud
"Perhaps you'd like to try."

I did just that, I ran on down,
And flew right through the air,
And when I reached that promised back,
The duck just wasn't there.

Instead, I made a belly flop
That hurt me quite a bit.
That haughty duck then spun about
And gave his head a flit.

"You silly little simpleton,
I said that you should try,
But if I meant I'd help you on,
I guess I told a lie.

"So next time, little fellow,
When someone seems sincere,
And offers you an easy ride,
Be sure that he'll be here."

I thought about what he just said,
And then I felt right sad,
If you can't trust what people say,
Then life might be all bad.

But then I paused a little time,
And thought what I had done.
I'd flow right through the empty air.
Is that what I should shun?

And yes, I'd made a belly flop,
But swam back to the bank,
And though I didn't get a ride,
At least I hadn't sank.

In fact, I'd had myself some fun,
And learned to take more care,
And though I'd had my troubles,
I'm glad that I was there.

And so I thanked the tricky duck,
And hurried on my way.
The next bird I encountered,
I know what I would say.

"Come hop upon my happy back,
And you can have a ride."
And when he did as I had asked,
To him I had not lied.

I'd carry him away with me
Until I reached my din,
To stuff him in my tummy,
So I'd be grinning then.

Revenge of the Over-the-Hill Parents

"How old are you now, just about five?
Now, that's a wonderful age.
When I was your age, my folks knew all.
When they spoke it was like words from a sage.
Since I knew almost nothing, and my brain wasn't old,
I always did as told—except what I did off stage.

"How old are you now, almost ten and three?
Now, that's a wonderful age.
When I was your age, my buddies knew all,
And all of us guys were on the same page.
And my parents knew nothing at all.
But that was sorta because, when I stayed out late,
I never managed to call.

"But now I am thirty-three, and I have a brat of my own,
And thirty-three, for parenting, *is not* a wonderful age.
Please, oh please, wise old parents, don't ever leave me alone.
I know I know almost nothing, and I'm not as wise as a sage,
And my child will listen to nothing, he's rebellious as he can be.
What will I do when he's older when right now he is only three?

"Oh my God, someday he *will* be older,
Too soon he'll be three and ten,
If I know almost nothing now, I'll know even less by then.
What will I do when his buddies and he are ganging up on me?
Oh if I had only listened to you when I was three and ten!"

"I hear you, my child, but I can't help but smile.
Yes, you too were once wild, and brought up my bile.
Though I sympathize now, there're no tears in my eyes,
Maybe I'll get back to you after a while.

18

"Ho, ho, hear me, all you over-the-hill parents,
And lustily laugh with me.
We were bound by our ignorance when younger,
But aging as set us free.
And now we have grandparent-fun, when we cannot lose
And our children can't win—
As the cycle of know-nothing parenting has started
All over again."

A Father's Love

Oh child of mine,
I'll make this pledge of love to you,
Throughout your life I'll be there by your side,
And though you leave and fly away, as children do,
What e're you ask will never be denied.

For there is nothing in the world
Could change my mind,
And nothing that you'd do
Would leave my love behind
Where're you go, my love will seek and find.
Oh child of mine, a father's love is always blind.

Family Gathering

The family had gathered together,
The old, the middle, the young,
And many a danced was danced,
And many a song was sung.
And, oh, the food was delicious,
Though it led to many a groan,

Continued . . .

So we promised each bite was the last,
But nothing was left on the bone.
Then, finally, the agony of parting,
If only we'd just stayed away,
But we knew in our hearts it was hopeless,
We'd be back on our next holiday.

Giving Away a Daughter

Hear me, my precious Caylen,
On this your wedding day,
Knowing all that you mean to me,
Of course I can't give you away!

Too much of me would vanish
If you're not here by my side.
The emptiness in my aching heart
Would be more than an ocean wide.

And yet I know it's time to let go.
No matter what your absence will do,
My holding on would hold you back.

Though I know you will miss me too,
The wider world will gain
A woman who's no longer a child.

.

So enough, I will not complain,
Hear now your father has smiled,
And his latent wisdom has won,
Since his love has created *more* love.
So his fatherly work is done.

Dear Caylen, I do not lose your love,
Instead, I gain a new loving son.

Why Hast Thou Forsaken Me?

We seek forever the father who never existed.
Whether biological or universal, the being who bore us
Is the myth our childhood mind could never have resisted,
The being just beyond the sky, who ever waits for us.

Oh wondrous father, who I knew in childhood, are you mine,
First to worship, then to fear, and then to boldly ask
"How could you fail to know the answers you are denying?
You were my face of truth, but did you wear a mask?

"Where is the certainty I once had thought you knew?
Where is the hoped-for meaning that justifies the pain?
Father, why hast though forsaken me again?"
Then finally, it comes to me, in this you have been true—
You also worshiped one you thought created you.

Not My Parents!

How did you feel when you first learned your folks
Were doing the old dirty deed?
And they didn't do it so you could come through it,
When your Mom's ready egg met your Dad's eager seed.

What your buddies told you just couldn't be true,
That after the deed was done,
The didn't feel guilty, nor even feel bad,
They just had a whole lot of fun.

But I'll not blame them, or let my friends shame them,
But this, I swear will be true,
That even when older, and hard as a boulder,
It's a deed that I'll never do!

Love is Defined
As Nearly Devine or Out of Your Mind

Sharing about family may then lead to reflecting on what might have created family—love, of course. The easy part of love is romantic love, the undying intensity of passion that we are all were supposed to have experienced, and what our teenagers are currently demanding of one another. But this is an adult dinner party and we, perhaps reluctantly, realize that love is not all wine and roses.

Perhaps the wine is reacting too quickly, love is not too far removed from lust, and so lust may slip into the conversation eventually. So, as the salads are served, and savored, romance is first savored, then some bitter herbs show up in the salad, or then some overly sweet ingredients also may be tasted. So as to not altogether diminish your appetite, I have alternated the sweet with the not so sweet, and left the possible aphrodisiacs to the end.

Love as Bon Appetite

I don't love her, I devoir her,
She is food for my soul.
She is tasty as tidbits
But much better whole.
She is nourishing, not filling
Though I consume her each day.
Without her, I'm empty.
What more can I say,
My Appetizer, my Main Course,
I sup till I hurt,
But then can't live without
My Delicious Dessert.
Perhaps you will worry,
Since she means all to me,
That I will not share her,
They'll be none for thee.
But that is the thing
About loving each day,
When you're caught in its sway,
A little bit of love
Goes a very long way.

Emptiness

Pain hurts, anger disrupts, and sadness
Lies on your chest like a massive boulder.
But the emptiness caused by the loss of love
Is worse by far than all those above.
It hurts, disrupts, and crushes your chest,
And after you're tortured by all of the rest,
Emptiness is infinitely colder.

Bachelors be Wary

Oh boys, let us be wary!
This is a bit too scary,
For if we dare to tarry,
Someone named Jill or Jerry,
Will force us all to marry,
And all our bachelor fun
Won't have even begun.
So now it's time to run,
This truth I now declare
All bach-e-lors must beware!

Why Must I Feel This Thorn?

Why must I feel this thorn the gores my chest
And digs within to pierce my tender heart
And gnaws and gnaws and will not let me rest
And makes me long to set myself apart
And leave you there to suffer, as you may,
The agony that you alone should feel
Because you only give your love *your* way,
While others think your love is less than real?

So should I choose to weep along with you?
I warned you that your way would lead to woe.
Or should I let the thorn just pierce *you* through
Because you would not hear what you should know?
  Don't weep, my Dear, you will not bleed alone,
  My tender heart will never turn to stone.

I'm Pleasing Me Too

Since I've nothing better to do,
I spend my time pleasing you,
And when these dull days are through,
I wonder if you do this too.
And if this deception is true,
I've been foolish, and also have you.
If so, here's what now I will do,
Admit what I've done is untrue,
Then find something better to do,
And when that something is through,
Then I'll truly be pleasing you,
and this is far better to do,
Since I will be pleasing me too.

Being Nice Isn't Always Nice

Confidants confide, they have nothing to hide,
They share their innermost feeling.
Though one may feel shame, the response is not blame,
The results is acceptance and healing.

The problem arises when one sympathizes,
And is kind but not very truthful,
If the hurting ones heed, they'll no longer bleed,
But the confidant has failed to be useful.

Then those who revealed will not have been healed,
And next time should consider concealing.
The result of these lies could be acts that aren't wise
And words that are cruel and uncouth-ful.

Continued . . .

So listen my friend, and this comprehend,
I'm bearing my soul for your hearing,
If you don't tell the truth, you *will* be uncouth,
And your niceness will not be endearing.

Stretching and Talking

The more the stretch, the more the gain.
The more the strain, the more the pain.
So if I do the opposite,
The pain will come again, again.

The same is true, when addressing you.
If I talk at length I may get through.
But if I say what you should do,
You'll beat me till I'm black and blue,
And pain will come again, again.

Warm Winds in Winter

Warm winds in winter are memories of spring
When I had been happy with you at my side,
But warm winds torment me—your warmth is denied—
So I prefer those memories that *winter* winds bring.

Take Care in the Gender Jungle
It's dangerous out there in the gender jungle,
A carnivore is lurking in a pelt-tight skirt,
Bloody red lips hide a venomous tongue
And razor-shape weapons that can do more than just hurt.

So all you young males, who think you're so macho,
Preening your fur, the king of the hill,
Just wait till a female locks on to your haunches,
Though lions may be bigger—lionesses kill.

Kissing was a Sin

For she was young and pretty,
And I was young and handsome,
And moonlight lit her dazzling face.
But I was shy and awkward, and knew a kiss attempted,
Would only end in shame, and then disgrace.

And so the moon was wasted,
And lips were never tasted,
I claimed instead that kissing was a sin.
But now I'm old and ugly, and in my aching dreaming,
I long to feel just once the sin that might have been.

A Dangerous Passion

A dangerous passion has brought us to this.
It started with glances, and then came the kiss
That drove us to moments, then hours of bliss.

But after the passion, there came the great pain,
Those moments of rapture came not again.

But what then continued was sometimes okay,
Then sometimes was boredom, day after day.

So, was that great passion worth all of the pain?
If time could be conquered would we do it again?

The answer is certain, though passion meant pain,
There's no doubt we'd both do the whole thing again.

We needed the passion to give us the shove
That changed mere passion to a lifetime of love.

She Went Away

She went away, and yet I know that she
Had tried to stay. I missed her woefully.
Such was our fate, our time was sadly done.
It was too late before it had begun.
We'd meet again when time had past away.
I'd wonder then if love could last that day
And if that's when she'd come at last to stay.

A Road Not Taken

A road was not taken, and a kiss was not stolen,
Under a stairwell, out-waiting the rain,
And she was quite pretty, and her hair gloss golden.
And I was soar tempted—then up spoke my brain,
"Be careful, young player, think what might come after.
The kiss that might thrill you could shame you instead.
What could be amusing might end without laughter.
If kissing means promise, then you'll have misled."

As I hesitated, my chance to kiss her just flittered on bye.
Since, thank goodness, the rain had just started to die.
So the road wasn't taken, and a kiss wasn't stolen,
Though she was quite pretty, and her hair was gloss golden,
My future wouldn't hold her, since I told her goodbye.
I hadn't misled her, my lips did not lie.
But why, so long after, do I still wonder why?

Love's a Vessel on a Perilous Sea

Love is a perilous journey upon a wintry sea,
And as we brave the weather, I'm glad that you're with me.
Although I love you now, *and ever*, it wasn't always so—
Waves that break upon the bow have nowhere else to go.

I'm glad that treacherous weather,
And turbulent times have passed,
That waves are merely ripples, though we're still sailing fast.
I'll whisper only one regret, beneath this racing moon,
Our journey through this heaven will have to end too soon.

Let's enter calmer waters, and down our anchor cast,
Let's spend our time together and make each moment last,
Let's swim beside our vessel, within the sea's embrace,
Until we reach a shoreline and find a warmer place.
And though the journey's over, and time begins to slow,
The waves of love will mingle with no place else to go.

I Am a String Quartet

A harp is the tingling of raindrop
On mirror-still mountain lakes,
Each drop's a single note,
That flows with others, till a song awakes.

A violin's a soulful swallow
That swoops and soars in the sky,
Then swiftly drops to the level of trees
And alights with a whispering sigh.

A viola's the rustling of leaflets
When a forest is stirred by a breeze,

Its whispering voice sliding silkenly
Through the reverently silent trees.

And then there's the violoncello
That soothes with mellifluous sounds
And brings all the players together
In a rapture without any bounds.

And I am this quartet of strings,
And I play for the one that I love.
The music springs from my strung heart strings
As though strummed by the angles above.

And you are my only conductor,
Who leads from your podium on high,
And the music that flows from my body
Enchants other lovers nearby.

But we are alone in our garden,
And no one will hear your sweet sighs,
And no one will see what the players will do
As soon as the melody dies.

An Act of Faith in the Garden

What an act of faith is planting a garden,
As we scatter seeds on a frosty Spring morn.
How can we believe those small seed of hoping
Could bear cabbage, lettuce, or full stalks corn?

What an act of faith is the act of loving!
Does not fate thrust forth a perilous thorn?
How can we hope that the risk we are taking
Won't destroy our hope when something other is born?

But the fruits of our garden and our loving
Are reasons for living this risk-filled life,
The reason we labor as risk-taking gard'ners
And live long lives as husband and wife.

So we'll have faith, and continue our planting,
And our love-making will just carry on,
So the fruits of our garden and our loving
Will sustain us till our final Spring-dawn.

Maybe Night is Sometimes Day

You're the stubbornest person I every knew,
Black is black and white is white,
And there is no gray between night and day,
And even your right is always right.

And when I decide what I want to do,
You have to do it another way.
And when I insist, you're always pissed
And won't talk to me the rest of the day.

I have to admit sometimes it's true
That I am wrong and you are right.
But I must insist even though you're pissed,
That day is day, and it's never night.

But what the heck am I going to do?
You're not all bad, I'm not all good.
We've made it, together, through terrible weather,
So I wouldn't leave, though maybe I should.
Because good would be bad without you.

Beware of Angel's Hair

There's a fragrance in the air,
Filled will spice and sweetness,
From a tempting-angel's hair.
There's a kiss that's more alluring
Than the wine from ancient cellars.
Be on guard and have a care!
For a warmth will creep upon you
That will be your sure undoing
And no matter what you think,
You'll be drowning in your senses,
And her kiss will taste like Heaven,
And you'll die for one more drink.

or

There's a fragrance in the air,
Filled will spice and sweetness,
From a *fallen* angel's hair.
There's a breath that's more alluring
Than the wine from ancient cellars.
Be on guard and have a care!
For a warmth will creep upon you
That will be your sure undoing
And no matter what you think,
You will sip the wine of Satan,
Then you'll hear his mistress laughing
As you take your final drink.

What I Should Have Done

Longing for what was, or might have been,
My soul seeks solace from shame.
Had I but done what I should have done
I would not be buried in blame.
If chance will allow my love to be seen,
I'll do what I should have done,
And the darkness that blackens my heart and soul
Will fade in the light of the sun.

The Final Fatal Disease

Pathogens that enter the mouth
Have a tough time going deeper,
They burn in that acid orifice
Like frantic fleas in a flame.
It's the nose that's the portal for damage.
If I die from a germ or virus,
It's my nose that is to always to blame.

When I kiss you, my own potent kisses
Fend against your dangerous lips.
It's only when I sniff your intoxicating essence
That my defense against illness slips.
After that, my heart, my mind, and soul
Are open to just one tiny shove
To fall completely, now and forever,
Into a diagnoses of "Illness of Love."

Ah Love, Please Let Us Speak
After Edward FitzGerald and Mathew Arnold

Ah Love, please let us speak before we part
And soothe the words I said that broke your heart,
Say all before the dawn brings on the day,
So love and life will have another start.

Is this then not the awful way of it,
When careless words are like a candle lit
That flares into a flame so fierce and hot
It burns the hand that first the candle lit?

So let us snuff this foul and foolish fire—
Before the sun arises even higher,
Lie down with me and hear my loving words
To end your pain and kindle new desire.

Rose-Wishes
Some people wish on the stars,
And that's alright, I suppose,
I'd rather wish on a flower,
Perhaps a bright yellow rose.
For stars are all distant and cold
And you cannot smell them at all.
And flowers are blooming all Summer,
And you smell them right into Fall.

So if the wishes you're making
Too often fail to come true,
Star-wishes gave you nothing
While roses were smelling *for you*.

I Want To Be My Love's Perennial

I want to be my love's perennial,
But right now I'm her annual flower,
And other young annuals are catching her eye,
And I must use all of my annual power
To lure her back to my fragrant airs
Or she'll drop my blooms to the ground,
And when winter comes my love will forget
That my love was ever around.

So I want to be her perennial,
And each spring I will blossom anew.
And all winter long, she'll await my coming,
To do what perennial's do,
To explode in the spring to make her heart sing
All of the summer through,
Her forever lover, her ever returning,
Her always perennial,
Long-lasting Lover King.

Be Happy, Birthday Girl

Going from eight to nine,
Is a creepingly long way to go.
For when you are as young as eight,
Time goes so painfully slow.

But when you're fifty-eight,
Time doesn't seem to wait,
And fifty-nine arrives too soon—
It does not hesitate.

Continued . . .

At eight, you were oh so beautiful,
At nine you were twice as fair.
Though older at fifty-nine,
Your beauty will still be there.

I loved you not at eight or nine,
Time didn't work that way.
I only know, though you're fifty-nine,
My love is here to stay.

My Stolen Angel

Someone stole my little angel
From the garden in my yard.
Life without my porcelain darling
Will be sad and very hard,
But when I thought I had it bad,
There came along a handsome lad
Who stole my *living* angel too.
So now I've nothing left to give.
I swear I do not wish to live
Without my *live* angelic you.

Love's Child

If it were only true
That I could be with you
Forever and a day,
I'd still be here tomorrow morning.

Who cares what they would say,
Just let the donkeys bray.
The thing that we would do
Would overcome their scorning.

And at the break of day
We'd bow our heads to pray
That love would see us through,
And then some promised morning
Love's child would be a-borning.

In Dreams

In dreams, I can move like the wind,
O're mountains, down valleys, through trees.
In waking, I can only pretend,
And my windstorms are barely a breeze.

In dreams, I can fly like a bird
And travel from Equator to Poles.
While waking, such flights are absurd,
And I travel no farther than moles.

In dreams, I'm a movie star's peer,
And women fall down at my feet.
While waking, they just snicker or jeer.
As a lover, I'm not famed, I'm effete.

In dreams, I'm a leader of men,
My voice is a clarion call.
In waking, my voice is so thin,
That I squeak, and no one listens at all.

In dreams, I live by my rule,
Always to myself I am true,
While waking, I'm a child still in school,
And I do what the other kids do.

Continued . . .

In dreams, I am all I can be,
There's no challenge I won't undertake,
When waking, I'm nothing but me,
And when challenged, I quiver and quake.

In dreams, I am all of these things—
That vanish when night is not there,
And though I don't travel on wings,
In waking, I don't really care.

In dreams, there is one thing not there,
A thing that is more than a dream;
In waking, all my dreams are like air,
And they vanish just a quickly as steam.

And that thing, I am here to declare,
Is a thing that will always be true,
That makes waking where I'd rather be.
And that's where you'll always be you,
Who *accepts me* for just being me.

I Told My Truth

I told my truth. Yes, it wasn't what you expected,
And now you're hurting. I could have carefully selected
My words to keep you mystified,
But then, eventually, you'd have to know that I had lied,
And though I'd charmed you for a while,
I'd end up un-respected.
And so I told my truth, for it's a friend I want to be.
I don't believe that truth should make an enemy.
If this is not *your* truth then, honestly,
Don't waste your time on me.

Frozen Love

I will mount Mount Everest,
And further rise above,
If I can scale your anger
And thaw your frozen love.

I'll Adore You

Give your heart a chance
To know what the moment will bring.
Give our love a chance
And hear how the angels will sing.
If this moment is ours,
I'll do the most wonderful thing—
I'll adore you.

Offer me a kiss
And I will be yours throughout life.
Leaving me without love
Would wound worse than a dull piercing knife.
Enter now my arms
And be all I'll need in a wife,
I implore you.

When our journey's done,
And life's given all that it will,
I'll be there at your side
And holding and loving you still,
Kiss me once again,
And I'll give you more than a thrill—
I'll adore you.

Love's a Revolving Door

A revolving door is a marvelous tool.
If you slip in just right, it won't be too tight,
And you'll quickly slide right through to the store.

But the trouble is when you get caught in its spin,
And go round and round like a fool—
Then find your fool-self right out on the street again.

A relationship may also revolve, going around and around.
If you ride it just right, it will be a delight,
And the warmth of love will unfold.

If you don't take a chance, and risk a romance,
Then no love will ever be found—
Then you'll revolve right around, outwardly bound,
And out in the cold again.

Heaven Has Turned Into Hell

Heaven has turned into Hell,
Someone I loved has died.
I thought I had always laughed,
Now I know I have always cried.

No one on Earth can replace her.
So why should I even try.
The only way to climb out of my Hell
Is pretend that she did not die.

But my mind won't let her leave me,
And my heart continues to bleed.
Even Earth is Hell without her,
And Heaven won't hear when I plead.
So I guess it is Hell that I need.

Night Whispers

When the warm wind whispers at night,
With the leaves as its vocal chords,
I hear words in multiple voices
Sung by elfin ladies and lords,
Or by silken voices of Sirens
Or by angels praising love in their choir.

And my heart is stirred by the music,
As the wind whispers words of desire,
And I wish for the love who has left me,
To feel what I feel on this night,
To hear the words of enchantment
And know of the promised delight,

To know that the elves and the angels,
And the Sirens that haunted the sea,
Have promised a path into Heaven
If she'll only come back to me.

But all I hear is the whisper
Of a sighing of wind through the trees.
And the voices of immortal beings
Are no more than a mournful breeze.

Then the winds subside with the dawning,
Then all that I hear is a moan
From the vocal chords of a mortal
Who must face the long day alone.

My Brain Falls in Love

My limbic system is too often unused,
While I live on top of my brain,
Where my frontal lobes are doing their thing,
And keep me from going insane.

While my far left lobe's calculating,
My right lobe is languishing behind,
The result of this efficient functioning
Is truly a Spokish-like mind.

Then all of a sudden, I break out of the mold,
When my occipital lobes imprint a vision of you.
Then my left-functioning lobe at last loses hold,
And my unused right lobe is as free as a child,
As my limbic system suddenly goes wild,
And instinctually I do what a wild child will do,
Without any thinking I am falling for you.

I am the Classroom Clown
I'm always the classroom clown,
All laugh at my lopsided grin,
'Cause I see the world upside down.
Though I'm fat, but I call myself thin.

That's how I make them all like me,
I laugh at myself and not them.
They think that I'm always happy,
"Cause no matter what, I'm not grim.

But I know that I'm carefully hiding
The person who is actually me.
The truth that I'm never confiding
The me that I won't let them see.

But you are the one I would know me,
Who sits by me every day.
If I just had the courage to show thee,
You, maybe, would hear what I say.

But even with you, I am clowning,
It's only when we are apart,
And I am not upside-downing,
That I show you my bleeding heart.

But in class I don't show my feelings,
Or thoughts that I won't dare to say
'Cause you'll laugh at what I'm revealing,
And your laughter would drive me away.

Of course, you'll think I am faking
So again, I'll pretend to be thin.
And then while my poor heart is breaking,
I'll just be your fat fool again.

A Train Whistle at Night

There's nothing that saddens me more
Than a train whistle moaning at night.
Perhaps it's because, like the train I am sleepless
And wistfully awaiting the light.

When I first heard that whistle, when I was yet young,
It sounded so lone and forlorn
It was though it cried out and begged to be loved,
Or wished it had never been born.
And young, as I was, the sound also said,
Someday you could lose your love too.

Continued . . .

Just suppose in the morning, your parents have left you,
Then what on this earth would you do?

And now that I'm older, the train has returned,
And the sadness I felt's come again,
And the loss I feel now brings on as much pain
As the loss I was fearing back then.
And the old mournful whistle is reminding me now,
That when I arrive at the day,
The sadness that haunted me all through the night
Will still not have gone away.

But unlike the train, I'll remain awake,
And *my* morning may never arrive,
For unlike the train, I've no station to reach,
And thus no reason to still stay alive.
The aloneness I hear in that sad sounding whistle
Is the same that I feel in my long night of pain.
For the sound that's receding now tells me *you're* leaving,
And will never come home again.

Love is an Obsession

When first we met, you ignited my fears.
I knew you would haunt me down through the years.
It wasn't your beauty. Beauty's a prize
That's sold in a market where everyone buys.
It wasn't your planning, your devious ways,
I was too clever to be lost in your maze.
It wasn't your anger, those few times I'd win,
Or knowing it would seldom ever happen again.
It wasn't the pain of your takeaway smile.
That smile would return in a torturous while.

It wasn't my knowing that you'd love if you could.
It was knowing, even then, that I understood
That all of these fears you ignited in me
Were how you would love any enemy,
And you had chosen to make me that foe
That you'd love forever and never let go.

But now you *have* left, and I no longer have fears.
I've endured your strange loving down through the years
So, what is this sobbing that everyone hears?
Your final leaving has ignited my tears.

Why, Why, Why!

When asking why I laughed, you sought an explanation?
The anger on your face looked more like *accusation!*
I'll tell you why I laughed if you truly wish to know,
But first I'd better duck, here comes another blow.

I'd gladly answer why, and give an explanation,
But with each accusation, I just feel desperation.
Instead, Ill tell you *how* to strengthen our relation—
Never ask me why, *request instead an explanation!*

Please Do Not Accuse

Please, oh please don't accuse,
I can learn, please just inform.
Please do not attack me like a swarm of bees,
For you'll bring me to my knees as you storm
My fragile brain, causing intracranial harm.
Please, set my sore mind at ease—
Please, oh please don't accuse!

Hope for a Homophobic

Don't run away, my love is not gay,
All love is not doomed to be lust.
I'm as straight as the side of a right triangle.
It's not rapture before you I dangle,
But a caring that lives only in trust.
I am offering the wisdom of sharing
And a love that won't whither away.

The Folly of Melancholy

Yes, I could be sad,
Bad things have occurred,
The love I thought I offered
Was not what you had heard.

And when you turned away,
I thought my life was done
Love, I thought forever,
Never had begun.

What lesson have I learned?
Don't live in fantasy.
Love that's never started
Is love that cannot be.

When phantom love has parted,
Don't cry, instead be jolly.
Don't fall into the folly
Of phantom melancholy.

Byron Redux

After I left, I didn't cry.
That's when I knew
I had said goodbye.
Love that is given
With certainty
And then rejected
Can set you free.

So give up the good
Along with the bad.
Regret turns the good
Into something sad.
Think of this parting,
And what went before,
Not as closing
But opening a door.

All That Glitters

All that glitters is not gold.
All that's tarnished is not old.
All that's brazen is not bold.
All that's cherished shan't be sold.
What they ask, you must withhold.
Once you've fallen, truth be told,
You'll be tarnish, you'll be sold.
All who warmed you will grow cold.
You'll remember, when you're old,
All that glitters was not gold.

Maryann's Sadness

I wondered why you were sad,
And why, at the moment,
Your sadness was making me glad.
But then I remembered your smile,
Your smile that banished the sad,
So I guess I was glad at that moment
For I knew that soon I'd be glad.

I Will be There

When you call, I will be there.
I'll come to you, just tell me where.
Through day and night, I'll feel your need,
You need not hurt, you need not bleed.
The Earth may turn, yet I will stand
So you may build your promised land.
The stars may fall, I'll shelter thee.
You will be safe when you're with me.
When you need warmth, I'll cover you.
So you may sleep the whole night through.
When you need hope, I'll point the way
So you may reach a brighter day.

There's just one thing I will not do,
I will not force my way on you.
You've but to ask, and I will give.
But if you don't, I still will live.

And yet I fear, the time will be
When you will need someone who's me.
And when you seek to see my face,
I will be in another place.
And when you cry and call for me,
I'll only be a memory.

I'm Leaving for Another Land

I'm leaving for another land,
I'm sorry, I didn't mean to leave so soon.
But I don't belong on this side anymore,
Soon I'll be crossing the Rio Grande.
But it's not into Mexico I'll be going,
Though the river is certainly as wide,
It's the journey beyond life's border
That awaits me on the other side.

So when you decide *you'll* be leaving,
That a land without me is too sad,
Just remember this departing old man
Was once your loving sweet lad.
And your handsome young husband is waiting
To welcome his eager young bride.

Somebody Stole a Kiss!

"Somebody stole a kiss!"

"I don't know what you're talking about."

"Don't give me that, you thief in the night,
I recognize your firm lip prints, now it's near light."

"I don't know what you're talking about."

"All right, I'll test you, I'll turn out the light.
If you're not being naughty, you'll do what is right."

"I don't know what you're talking about."

"You'll give back the kiss that you stole from me,

Then you'll give me another, and that one for free.
Then the lights will stay off so no one will see
What else you might decide you will give to me."

"I confess, I confess, the truth has won out,
Now truthfully I know what you're talking about!
So turn out the light so I can make good,
And give you what else you think that I should."

Do Not Mock My Fallen Blade

What is this foolish thing you do,
You mock my fallen blade
That recently has pierced you through
To end my midnight raid?

You think my blade won't rise again
To be a steel-hard shaft,
And I won't thrust it in again,
But this time, fore and aft?

And do not think your flimsy shield
Will brush aside my blade
I'll pen you down upon the field.
Oh then your smile will fade!

If not, before the final thrust,
Beneath me you will kneel
And kiss the blade, as kiss you must
My blade now hard as steel.

And then my blade will have its day,
And laughing in your eyes,
My blade will send you on your way—
This time to Paradise.

In Praise of Hoary Latin Poets

Those old Latin poets were amazing,
They knew all we know in our day,
And they wrote in glorious rhythms
And in forms that have shown us the way.
They composed great odes and epics
Putting our puny poems to shame,
That even in modern translation
Justifies brilliantly their fame.
There was Horace, and Ovid, and Virgil,
And Lucretius—the noblest of men—
Who proudly extolled Roman virtues—
But were also as licentious as sin.

But Catullus was the one who was famous
For shocking readers, yet never, never boring 'um,
His poems were often so smutty,
He must have copied them in a smelly devacatorium.

What follows in not a translation,
But what Catullus the Smutty might have said
As he tore off his old sweaty toga,
And slipped into another man's bed.

"Lift up your treasure-hiding hemline,
And show me the ruby beneath,
And soon I will caress with my fingers
And nibble what I find with my teeth."

And then that lady surprised him,
She lifted her dress up her thighs,
And exposed the jewel in his lust he'd devour
With his eager, lascivious eyes.

But just as he fell to his trembling knees
To savor a closer look,
Her luscious legs snapped together again,
No longer an open book.

Then he realized to his horror
And his old-man shame,
In his passion, he had named her Lesbia,
Which wasn't the fair lady's name.

So that is the end of this story,
The poem that old Catallus might have writ,
And probably not half as dirty
And with only a touch of his wit.
But like that long-vanished poet,
I know also when I should quit.

I'm Warmer Than Cold

As I grow old, love has become problematic.
Remember those days
When my glands made me crazed
And loving was automatic?
Nowadays, when reaching for rapture, I'm amazed
When any lust makes the scene.
Then the best I can do
Is last till I'm through,
Cause quitting is not very keen.

Well, Lover, there's one consolation,
I'll provide you at least one sweet sensation.
Though great when first wed
Now that I'm old,
I'm still warmer than cold—
So I'll *warm* you when I lie in your bed.

Love 'Um or Leave 'Um

Love 'um or leave 'um
But do not deceive 'um.
Don't pretend to care
When the love isn't there.
In the end you'll only grieve 'um.

I Climbed Ice Mountain

I climbed Ice Mountain.
The way was perilous, the risk was great.
Furious winds buffeted my body,
Icy handholds were as jagged as hate.

I climbed Ice Mountain.
My breath was ragged, I gasped with the strain.
My arms were aching, my flesh was frozen.
Why was I willing to do this again?

I climbed Ice Mountain.
My courage faltered, but I wouldn't stop.
The goal to be gained was worth my hoping,
In spite of my agony, I would reach the top.

I climbed Ice Mountain.
You mightn't think that would matter much,
But when I surmounted your furious feelings,
You melted 'neath my warm caring touch.

* * *

I've a hole deep down in my tummy,
Though I've stuffed it with grub from above.
It's not food that must fill that vast cavern,
It needs to be stuffed with your love.

55

56

When All Else Fails
Laughter Prevails

Perhaps we went a little too far into lust-land, so while we await the entrées, we call upon humor to hide the embarrassment. Laughing at one's self is the safest humor, although in mocking ourselves we might be attacking what we actually abhor in others. I do both, of course, and so I've tried to alternate the "I'm really OK" with the "You're not OK's," although it turns out I have written more of the making-fun-of-others poems.

But, no matter how debonair, underneath all of the I'm-above-it-all lurks the truth—whether angry or lighthearted, this poetic humorist is a closet moralist, using all of his poetic devices to try to change the world into something he believes is good rather than something he fears is bad.

Enjoy the light repast. My guess is, you'll taste yourself somewhere in the poetic tidbits I am offering.

For the Rest of My Boringish Days

Evil's done, now virtues begun,
But I have to admit, evil was fun,
But I have to abandon my old evil ways,
For the rest of my boringish days,
Or the Devil will bake off my bun.

All That's Mine is Yours

I give this pledge to thee,
All that's mine is yours.
I'll never even ask
You give it back to me.
Although, I must confess
It causes some distress
That, though my pledge endures,
All that's yours is yours!

At Least Appreciation

Of course, I'd like more money, and even more adulation,
And I'd like to believe you think I'm truly a super-sensation,
But when I do what I think is right, and others color me
black,
And gather in angry crowds to stretch me over the rack,
I hope that you, at least, will be standing by
With some words of consolation
And if not with outspoken respect and at least some
appreciation.

Hyper From Hell

When she skips her morning coffee,
My wife's a Hyper from Hell,
But even her cups of caffeine do not break the hyper spell.
So I'm forced to funnel down my throat a vat of potent brew
So her hyper rant and ravings
Don't make *me* coffee-hyper too.

In Praise of Our Essence

What is more human than the human fart?
The brain may be wise,
And love for our children may be born in the heart.
But we are what we eat, and that has its start
In the human body's open upper part,
Which is also used, you've realized,
For the language that makes you more humanized.
And speaking and eating, wherever they start,
Will finishes their job at the end of the cart—
Where what is more human than the human fart.

Yes But

I'd love to hear you say, "Yea, yea,
Of course you're not a nut."
But then you almost always say
The terrible, "Yes, but. . ."

A Word to the Wise

A word to the wise should be sufficient,
But the wise aren't away so wise.
Especially if they know somewhat less than they think,
Then they're in for a painful surprise.

So listen to those who might be less wise
But who tell *themselves* no lies
Because their egos are not so inflated,
And they know what they know
And thus may have more to show
Than those whose wisdom's too overrated.

Adult Mockery

Who are these children, masquerading as adults,
Driving SUV strollers, with calamitous results,
Playing childish games as though they're really life,
Pretending to me married, a husband and a wife,
And, worst all, deceiving no one but themselves,
Claiming they are parenting, but all their kids are elves?
Who are these silly children, this adult mockery?
Look into the mirror, you'll see there you and me.

Fat Car!

Fat car, fat car,
Why must you guzzle so many gallons of gas?
Sorry to be so crass,
But your booze is costing so much money
I am taking it up the ass.

Only Laugh at Yourself

Laugh at yourself
And the world laughs with you,
Laugh at another and he'll spit in your face,
And he'll call you an evil elf
And shout that it isn't your place
To force him to look at himself.
And he'll sue you if ever you do.

Irony

My irony will be the death of me
For I'm making fun of my betters.
For my lack of respect,
They will chop at my neck
And leave my bare bones bound in fetters.

People Who Like Me

I only like those who also like me,
All others can go their own way.
That way, I won't have to be
Spending the livelong day
Always trying to sway
Other to like the wonderful me
That they somehow never see
Because stupidity gets in their way.

In the Movies

I cry when the actors are crying.
I cry when hearing their song.
I cry when the actors are happy,
I cry when things go all wrong.

Perhaps that makes me a weakling,
And my feelings would control what I do,
And I wouldn't do what was needed—
Well, I assure you that just isn't true.

Crying might be just what's needed
To know what a hero must do
To save all his people from crying,
And you might be one of those too.
So why don't you go to the movies
To cry where no one will see,
And then when you find that I'm crying,
Perhaps it's you who'll save me.

Ticks of Terror

A tiny tick is one tough terror.
You can smash it or squeeze it,
You might even freeze it—
It'll dig in and still keep biting.

Our foes are big ticks of terror.
Though they might not like the comparison,
Even when they're on the run,
They burrow in and keep on fighting.

Continued . . .

To avoid either ticks of terror
Stay away from where they hide,
You can't wait till they all have died.
Being bitten continiues uninviting.

Wealthy Work

I've come again to where I spent my time
With friends with wealth, while I knew poverty.
But as a boy I hoped that I would climb
Above my station and my misery.

And so I spent my days in lowly work
While wealthy friends did little more than play,
I thought them born to lead, and I to clerk.
They'd rise on wealth while I must earn my way.

But lowly labor had its just reward,
I earned my food, and challenge stretched my mind,
And thus my *mental* work was seldom hard.
Now I've returned, and left that shame behind.

And I'm a doctor now, with wealthy work—
A former wealthy friend is now my lowly clerk.

Audition

"How long is long?"

"When long's too long
Or Long's all wrong,

I'll ring the gong.
Until that time
Just sing your song. . .

Gong! Gong!

"What's wrong?"

"Your song's all wrong
And far too long!"

"But just one note
Has left my throat!"

"We know—
That's why it's time you go!
Gong! Gong!"

Terminal Ticks

Having ticks on your testical
Is far from being restical.
But very much more hectical
Is ticks way up your rectical.

Work

Sometimes I would do it, sometimes just work at it.
Or hammer and screw it, or work as a clerk at it,
Or plant it then chew it, or stab with a dirk at it,
Or fry it or stew it, though customers up-chirk at it,
I'd chisel, then on-view it, though critics all smirk at it.
I'd learn till I knew it, or fail it then irk at it,
I'd dance or Kung fu it, and pirouette or just jerk at it
I'd catch as they threw it, and stay in the game at it,
Denying I knew it, I'd sign a fake name at it,
Then legally eschew it, thus gather no shame at it,
Sometimes I might rue it, sometimes, I'd just blame it.
Sometimes when I blew it, I'd be awful sad at it,
But then I'd poop-poo it, who cares if I'm bad at it.

At last, I'd get through it—in this, I'm emphatic—
And then I'd undo it, because I'm no work addict.

Urinals Know

Urinals now know when you're done.
As soon as you've finished your play,
The water comes gushing down
And washes your urine away.

I also know when *you're* finished.
When you've said all you are going to say,
I flush all you've said from my mind
And relieved, just go on my way.

White is Black

"I tell you, this is white."

"No, it's not, it's not!"

"It's white, just use your sight."

"No it's not, it's black!
And it was black a long way back.
You think that I'm not bright?

"It's not your brains that I attack.
You'll know that I am right
If you just use your sight."

"No, no, I'll never look!
I tell you, in my book,
It's always been all black.
It's you that has the lack
Of using intellect.
It's black, it's black, it's black!"

"Oh what the heck,
Although you're out of whack
Okay, okay, it's black."

Leader's Lament

Give me back my power, I always led you before.
I always knew so much more than you,
And now I know even more.
So just because you're older doesn't mean
You should show me the door.
Just give me back my power,
And our lives will go on as before.
Besides, there's one thing more, *old* fellow—
Remember, you *are* only four!

Golf Carts

Golf carts are for old fat farts
Who will not walk the course,
Who'd never stroll from hole to hole—
They'd rather face divorce.
For that's the way the game is played,
It is a *manly* sport,
And if you doubt their manly-hood,
"Then have it understood,"
They cleverly would snort,
"You're only envious
Because you are too poor
To play our rich man's sport."

* * *

Rain, rain, go away,
I don't like your wet sensation.
Come again some other day
When someone else is on vacation.

Get Out of My Face

Get out of my face,
Do not enter my space
This is my special place
To be with me.

Just come back again,
And only now and then,
And also *only when*
I'm needing company.

Painted Beauty

What am I seeing? What does it mean?
Are you a beauty or merely obscene?
Your face is so coated with layers of paint,
You could be a harlot, you could be a saint.
And whatever beauty that somehow seeps though,
Is it just from a manikin or really from you?
But I'm just a man and not 'sposed to know
What lies beneath that cosmetic glow.
I'm just to be thankful to be in your thrall,
And love you forever—and pay for it all.

Why am I Always Thinking?

Why am I always thinking when it causes me so much pain?
Why don't I just live meditating, avoiding the endless strain?
Why can't I just be a larva, enjoying my time in the hive?
I guess it's because when I'm thinking
At least I know I'm alive.

The New Satan

The truth is finally known, ancient evil's come again,
Satan is the internet, lurking in his fetid pit,
Spreading forth temptation, advertising wanton wares,
Sucking in his sinners with his seductive, evil wit.

Call upon your Maker! Put your brain into His hands.
Let Him teach you abstinence, although it brings you gloom.
Never mind the afterlife, for you'll live your hell on Earth
If you spend your foolish self into certain fiscal doom.

The Poem of the Plaintive Pessimist

Why, why, Why?
Why can't I do whenever I try?
Why don't people just listen to me?
Why don't they care when I cry?
Why don't they answer my plaintive plea?
Why don't they understand
Though I'm living today,
Someday I surely must die?
Why are they standing by
While foul fate is awaiting me?
Why are my nights such misery?
Why is life like a horrible dream?
Why doesn't awaking just set me free?
Why am I always less than I seem?
And mostly why, why, why
Do I continue to ask the repetitive "Why?
When the answer is obviously
Merely stop asking "Why, oh why?"
And be!

Heels Over Head

My heart gave a start,
You know how it feels,
So I fell out of bed,
Head over heels.
But that is a strange thing to do.
When you think it through,
It makes more sense,
When you tumble hence,
That you're heels over head
When you fall out of bed.

Government Spam

Choctaw Charly and Shawnee Sam
Were sitting cross-legged on the hot desert sand.
Sam asked of Charly, pointing his hand,
"What's that you're eating, leftover Spam?"

Charly replied, disgust in his voice,
"I eat what they give me, they give me no cash.
My Government rations are better than trash,
But I'd sooner eat buffalo, if I had a choice."

Then Sam said to Charlie, a smile on his face,
"Yes, those were the days when we rode the great race!"
Then his smile turned to sadness, and pain froze his face.
"Too bad it all ended in this place of disgrace."

Then Choctaw Charly and Shawnee Sam
Closed their sad mouths and said nothing more.
And the desert grew colder than ever before,
And Charly didn't finish the rest of his Spam.

What is it Like?

What is it like to linger in poverty,
When others are wallowing in wealth?
What is it like to be ill and in pain,
When others can pay for their health?
What is it like to be told that you're bad
And only the wealthy are right?
What is it like to be told you're insane,
When you get so angry you fight?
And is it surprising the wealthy complain
When you win the battle you start?

And, you, who are wealthy,
Are you feeling the strain,
Does it pain, does it smart?
And what is it like to no longer have wealth?
Poor thing, you are breaking my heart!

Supermarket Seduction

Get 'em when they come in the door,
Pile the goodies from ceiling to floor.
After you greet up, then make 'em eat 'em.
Though of health you'll deplete 'em.
If they're moaning, just beat 'em
Then shove 'em all out of the old Final Door.
And don't worry, there'll always be more.

* * *

The Orangutan is so like us,
The Creationists must wear a truss.
But considering all we humans do,
Primates like them are mortified too.

The News is Not Fun Anymore

The news is not fun anymore,
We're no longer wining our wars,
Everyone in the world now hates us,
And there's not even life on Mars.
And it's just as well that there isn't,
For the Martians would hate us too,
For sending them creepy-crawlers
Cluttering their unpolluted view.
I guess I could listen to radio
But, there, rappers are ranting with hate,
So I guess I'll just listen to newscasts,
And accept that news is my fate.
At least the news is so horrible
It makes reality TV second rate.

Pompous Person, Blow Your Horn

Pompous person, blow your horn
Act as though you own the road.
All I see behind that wheel
Is just a fat and foolish toad.
I hope that when your drive is done
You'll sink again down in your fen
And be what you have always been,
A toad that occupied the road
With other noisy toads
Pretending to be men.

Super Spies Are Never Alive

Characters in spy novels are always diabolically smart,
Who are weaving their way through a convoluted story
Contrive by paranoid authors, stretching the novelist's art,
So you never know who is evil and who should win all the glory.

Our real-life spies are just human and pathetically human as well,
And our fabulous agencies of spying are made up of fallible folk
Who foul up files on computers, and hope that the voters can't tell.
To them, the novelist's hero is really no more than a joke.

Since the enemy is also no smarter, I guess reality's not bad—
Until their mistakes cause disaster, and all the world turns to dust.
So I guess the secret's not spying. If we ever hope to be glad,
We must open our hearts to all others,
And finally learn how to trust.

What You Deserve

I learned a lesson today.
Disappointment has haunted me.
I had a plan, it should have worked
I cut no corners, I never shirked.
Everything just went astray.
Old fickle fate had flaunted me.

First, I felt it wasn't fair,
If you do right, *you do deserve!*
What I had done, all said was right,
Like black is black and white is white.
But here's the lesson I must share—
You might not get what you deserve.

The Accumulation Nation

I wish I had more money,
I'd spend it on myself.
I'd buy a bunch of things,
And put them on my shelf.
Of course, I would not use them,
I'd have no need for them,
I hadn't planned to buy them,
Their purchase was a whim.
And after several sessions
The shelf would grow too small,
I'd shove them in my closets
Until I'd filled them all.
At last, there'd come a time
There'd be no space for more,
I'd sell them all on eBay,
And head back to the store.

Perhaps you think it foolish
To spend your time this way,
But this is how we do things
Is good old USA.

Piddlely-Poop

What's in the soup?
Oh, piddelly-poop,
The same old goop,
Oh well, oh hell,
Scoop me a scoop.
What starts as soup
Will then descend
To in the end
Be piddlely-poop.

Cavemen Have Come Again

What is this noise that rebounds through the house?
Where is Beethoven and where is Strauss?
What poses as singing could come from a hog,
And the rhythm's a bone that's pounding a log.
The ascendance of music is no longer in,
And the cave man within us has now come again.

The Mortal Sin is Counterproductive

If you live in sin, there is no repentance,
Your later good deeds will not lighten the sentence.
So the Catholics proclaim, with their *mortal* sin,
So my protest, like Luther's, on the church door I'll pin—
I'd at least like *one* chance to start over again—
Since a sinning Catholic has no way to win,
He might as well keep sinning, again and again.

King John

Here's King John upon his throne.
Hear him bellow, hear him moan.
If he shouts one more complaint,
Though I'm patient as a saint,
With a stone I'll grind his bone.
Then he'll moan there all alone.
So, Old King John, get off your throne!

Moaning at Home on the Rig

I have my reason to quit this season,
It is not pleasing me.
My butt is freezing, my nose is sneezing,
My lungs are wheezing,
And I long to sail back over this sea
To a land where the weather
Brings holly and heather,
And I float like a feather.
It is there that I'd rather be.
Instead I am stuck here,
And all out of luck here—
But I'm making a buck here
On this oily cold northern sea.

Abstinence-cy

Papa, don't torture me
Release me from my abstinence-cy,
If I slip up and kiss,
That moment of bliss
Might mean naughtiness
That I cannot resist,
And your folks will insist
That I cease and desist,
Or it's in the abyss
I'll receive my next kiss
From the Devil's hot fist.
So, Papa, please set me free
From living in abstinence-cy.

Continued . . .

You will? Oh Papa, Papa, I really thank Thee.
Though, now I'll confess, I've been a bit free.
Oh hell, Oh hell, now I'm unable to pee!
It's time I reconsider
Practicing abstinence-cy.

It May Be Wise to Sympathize

What's happening to the other fellow
Isn't worth too much of a mention.
If you thought it could happen to you,
You might pay more careful attention.
Of course, if the other fellow is hurting,
You no doubt could *empathize*,
But if his pain then started *you* hurting,
You might slip up and sympathize.
Putting yourself in another's position
Makes it likely you will realize
If you dare to care for another
Y*ou* then might be the one who cries.
So it's wiser to hide in indifference.
Don't care, don't love—just despise.
Don't encourage, don't reward, don't praise,
It's safer to criticize.
That way, you won't feel lonely
When anyone you might care for even dies.
On the other hand,
If you ever expect to be happy,
You are in for a painful surprise.

Types of Cars

There are toy cars for tiny boys
And boys a whole lot older.
There are tank cars for macho boys,
Who are trying to look a lot bolder.

There are green cars, low gasoline cars,
For those trying to be a lot wiser.
I like green cars, lean gasoline cars,
But only because I'm a miser.

Two Kinds of Worms

If you open a can of worms,
Something and someone squirms—
Wiggly worms don't like the light,
And guilty people prefer the night.
Worms become an angler's bait,
People who sin must meet their own fate.
But even if the lid's replaced
In time, the worms will die.
And people who've lived a lie
Will have to feel disgraced.

At least the worms will be of use,
They are food that will turn into fish,
And from fish to an angler's dish.
Can sinning people be also of use?
No one wants to dine on them.
Should we then just let them swim?
No, we should never turn them lose,
For if we let facile fish off the hook,
They'll hide again in the can.

Continued . . .

So maybe there's a better plan,
To flop these fish in a frying pan
And fry them till they stink like hell
Then they might learn this lesson well—
If you're a liar, you are going to smell.

My Razor Broke

My razor broke. In one quick stroke,
I changed from an urbane cavalier,
To a bearded beast, who could rise like yeast,
To hang from a chandelier.

What more would it take if one small mistake
Could make me one you'd despise,
An ancient beast, so long deceased,
Whose vaunted intellect won't again rise?

I am glad that I, who cannot fly,
Have feet firmly fixed on the ground,
Who can go to the store and enter the door
Where an unbroken razor can be found.

You're Not God's Steeple People

Power people beneath the steeple,
It's time to potentiate the process of peace!
What makes war always inevitable is a painful decrease
In the world's resources,
While populating goes on without cease.
If God intends for His folks to survive,
We must cease our senseless breeding,

And those who preach against ways to decrease
The results of this sinful exceeding
Are only impeding the process of peace
By increasing the populations
Of those nations who must go to war
To feed their starving relations.

It's time to be one of God's good neighbors,
And help Him reduce His labors.
If you can't really hear what He wants you to hear,
As unfortunately it would appear,
You're a part of the problem and one of those phony
And overly loud steeple people.

All's Well in Heaven

My brethren, we must do what's right,
For our own and all others as well.
We must care for those less fortunately born
Or we'll *all* end up in Hell.
Most of all, we must guard against anger,
Though it's true we're sometimes hated.
Don't worry, we'll receive our reward,
Because God's Heaven is segregated.

* * *

According to our Equal Rights Amendment,
All of our groups should be equal,
But, of course, it *actually* means,
None are really as equal
As America's lily white people.

South Florida, Heaven or Hell

South Florida winters are wonderful,
The days are sun-filled, and the nights are cool.
Who wouldn't want to live in such weather?
You'd be such a poor Northern fool
To live through the gray, soot-filled days
Of those dreadful Northern climes,
When living in a Florida winter
Is living in the best of times.

But to get through to December,
And then on to Heaven,
One must live through the hellish end of summer,
When the day-heat's an oven,
And the nights are all sweaty,
'Cause the humidity's ever more of a bummer.

But what is even more dreadful—
And maybe even insane—
Is living in a Florida summer
During a late summer hurricane,
When the winds may blow
And howl through the night,
Shuttered windows may shatter,
And rooftops take flight,
And the ocean may rise
And flood through the house,
As you cling to your children and terrified spouse.

So there is the tradeoff—
Florida winters may be like a Heaven—
But late summers there can be living hell,
So choose your pleasure and choose your poison—
Oh, by the way, I've a house there I'm thinking to sell.

The Tropical Life

A tropical life without a wife
Is not so exotic as boring,
Unless you are willing
To go island-hopping
Wasting half of your life
A-whoring.

Bambi's Not Cute in Virginia

Bambi's not cute in Virginia,
He wanders my property in the wee morning hours.
His favorite entrée is my new vegetable garden,
And his favorite desert is all of my flowers.

You Disney-lovers, animal-lovers, and children,
I don't want to make you forlorn,
But the hunter should have shot Bambi's mother
Before her baby was born.

Dream Flying

In dreams, I can fly, but not very high,
But just below me the ground passes by.
From where I start out to way over there,
I just leave my feet and sail through the air.
I travel with ease, no hill is too steep,
I revel in speed, while other just creep
And I fly so fast, I win every race,
It's only when I wake that I fall on my face.

High Maintenance Wife

She's a high maintenance wife,
I'm a hardworking spouse,
She's a passel of virtues but her needs fill my house.
I'm asking this question, should I limit my life
To earn all those virtues
From this high maintenance wife?
Is she worth all the efforts, though our marriage I'd save,
If my efforts just lead to my premature grave?

Why Not Celibation?

Masturbation
Causes sensation,
And that's okay
In its limited way,
But it seldom creates
Creation.

And fornication
Makes its sensation,
And when it's done,
There is some fun,
But it often becomes
Masturbation.

To avoid temptation
Of mere masturbation,
Although it's no fun,
So it's seldom done,
The solution might be
Celibation.

Men Who Would be Kings

Some men are known to brag,
That when they ascend the throne
That they're still inclined to be erect
Instead of just pitifully prone.
I hope I don't offend, but alas I must contend
That some men are inclined to drop
When attempting instead to ascend.

To Write a Witty Poem

To write a witty poem,
There is a way to do it.
Find a thought that's stuck
Down in your mental muck
And cleverly unglue it.
For example, here's a prize:

My children never thought me wise,
They said my words were prattle.
But when they came to realize
I knew what I was at-al—
They sadly learned, to their surprise,
My brain was *now* too addle.
And here's one more you might adore:

I never knew a woman
Who though that I was good,
And when I tried to please one,
She said I never could.
But when I tried to squeeze one,
Can this be understood?
She said that I was good
And that I could and should.

Miami, Bye-Bye

When compared to wild Miami,
Where the life is *psychasthyny*
Life in Lynchburg's such a cinch,
Leaving here, I'd be a Grinch.

So Miami, please don't cry,
It is time we say goodbye.
Adios, Amigos. . .
And now, so long, bye-bye.

I've Been Raped by My HMO

I once was a virgin,
Till I broke my toe,
Then I went to the Doc
Who took some dough,
Then sent me on
To my HMO.
He fixed me fine,
But don't you know,
The HMO
Stretched me out supine
And struck such a blow
That they ruptured me
Somewhere down below.
Then they laughed in glee,
And then fiscally
Then deflowered me,
And took away
My virginity.

I choose Gallows Humor

I choose to use gallows humor
In the face of an un-benign tumor,
Then if my too terrible tumor
Is merely an un-benign rumor
Then those terrible nights
When fears might ascend new heights,
I'd be laughing so I couldn't be gloom-er.

Something's the Matter!

The power's out, something's the matter,
That's why I've climbed this ten foot ladder.

Okay, I'm on the very top
But it is just a little drop.

But I won't fall, I'm smart and able,
I'll grab a-hold of this cut off cable.

Oh yhipes!, oh hell, I could be wrong.
I hope my bottoms nice and strong!

I'm No Bird Brain

Birds find thousands of seeds
That they buried throughout the year.
I can't even find the keys to my car
When I know they ought to be *here*.

So when someone calls me a birdbrain
Who remembers just dittily-squat,
I thank them and then disagree—
That intelligent I am certainly not.

An Open Letter to TV Executives

Dear Madam or Sir:

I'm writing you this letter to tell you what I've seen. Or maybe I'm so angry I need to vent my spleen.

I saw a TV movie, where the hero sought revenge when a drunken driver killed the hero's lifelong friend. In a righteous rage, the hero bashed the drunken diver's skull, until the driver died from the beating he received.

Was the hero's violent binge something viewers should condone, just because our sorrow made us feel his anger as our own?

But then we learned the driver had lost his child and wife, and then his pain so warped his mind, for the first time in his life, he drank to drive the pain away, but drove instead his car right into the hero's friend.

How should this story end? Four peopled died, and two took lives that were not theirs to take. Then, when our hero came to realize why the driver drank so much, he felt such burning shame, he also sought to know oblivion, the way the drunk had done, until his drinking led, not to a speeding car, but to a loaded gun. And then the hero blew away his life— and now the dead were five.

So was the alcohol the cause of all this grief? Or is our alcohol just one more way us humans seek relief? And is our faulty humanness the thing that after all should bear the final blame?

To tell the truth, I just don't know, perhaps they're both the same. To truly be a human being, we care for those we love. And when we lose the ones we love, perhaps it's just the final shove that sends our frail humanity into a violent binge of fierce ancestral bestiality.

But Sir or Madam, all of this was not what caused my ire. The callousness of what came next just set my hate on fire.

The movie faded out, and then commercials owned the television screen. And how the sellers sought to sell was totally obscene. Two gorgeous youthful lovers were toasting their affair, by hoisting steins of alcohol into the smoke-filled air, as though their beer was just the way to make their loving bold. And then the camera left the bar and found a speeding car, and tried to tell the viewers that their macho road machine could reach such sexy speed they'd be a movie star.

Now neither ad said we should drive when we have had our drink. It's not their fault that when we drink we sometimes do not see the link between the fun of happy drinking and driving on the brink. But do not try to tell me that they don't know that when we drink their evil drink we often do not think.

So that is why I'm angry, and why I've let you know, I'm telling all my friends to skip your shameful TV show!

Nothing could be truer,
I am forever yours
A Very Angry Viewer.

Oh, by the way, I've one more thing to say, after exiting the bar, I hope you speed your life away in your brand new macho car.

* * *

All around, signs can be found
Proclaiming Washington slept in this town.
Does that mean that Washington was sleeping around?

* * *

I've loved all the gifts you've given,
You've given in every way.
But that was then, and this is now,
So, what have you given today?

If You Lead Us to War
We May Have Gone Too Far

The exchange of humor may have relaxed us enough to risk discussing that which is far less digestible than our excellent meal. Yes, we may still laugh at times, but when the conversation turns to war, it is gallows humor that we use to manage our emotions, our anger, and our fear.

I doubt that any of us are for war, but we might differ on its necessity. And if it is at times necessary, can we at least praise those who must suffer the most—our warriors, and especially our very young warriors? I certainly respect—and regret—their sacrifice, so most of this painful food for thought will taste more bitter than savory.

The Instruments of War

Oh what a clarion call the trumpet makes!
Stirring the hearts of all our young warriors.
Comrades are joined, valor awakes,
All is glory, war has no horrors,
No risks too great for honor of country
And the rights and protection of family.

But now that the dreadful battle has started
What instrument can sing the true sound
When the courageous die before the faint-hearted,
And the clamorous cacophony of a mortar round
Blasts the ears like an un-tuned timpani
And the stirring trumpet looses reality?

Then silence settles on the battle ground,
Where fallen warriors are unable to hear.
The trumpet returns with a new kind of sound,
Announcing that peace has vanquished the fear.
Hear now the taps at the end of the day—
But the valiant young warriors have all gone away.

No Victors in War
"I'm finished with war," the General said.
"At first I let victory go to my head
And only a few of my soldiers were dead.
But after the war, the hate we had bred
Promoted no peace—there was chaos instead.
So war has no victors. We generals had led
Till even the living all wished they were dead.
So I'm finished with war," the General said.

Was I a Knight in Another Life?

Was I a knight in another life,
Riding a great golden stallion,
Leading the charge of my warriors
Against a massive battalion?

And was I heroic, although a bit careless,
And my men saw me fall on the field,
And when the battle was over
Did they carry me off on my shield?

Did they cry that I died for my country,
My wife, my children, my home,
And across the skies with our heroes
Will my spirit continue to roam?

But I am alive in a modern age.
It's a pity but a hero I'm not.
I guess I will settle for doing
Whatever duties I've got.

But feel no shame for me, comrades,
The terrors you faced on *your* way
Were nowhere near as dreadful
As the horrors *we* face today.

Though I'm not a Medieval warrior,
If I just will stand here and fight
I'll conquer *a few* of those horrors
Before I fade into night.

So I guess in the light of this challenge
You should shout forth your clarion call,
In the face of our now-a-days evils
I am truly a hero after all.

Our History of War

In war's history, could there ever be
A more terrible century?
The First, The Second, The Korean,
And then The Viet Nam.
And what have we learned through each tragedy?
To kill all the people we don't even need The Bomb.
And what do we face in this new century,
When no enemy is lurking on the far frontier?
We are the enemy, and if we're ever to win,
We must conquer the enemy that lurks within.
And what is the cause of this threat to our land?
Our appetite for hating what we don't understand.

What Right Is

"Yes, I would fight and even die
For what I know is right."

"But who can say what right is?"

"I always know, it's in my bones
Just as I know what a day or night is."

"But I too claim the right to know,
For example, what delight is."

Continued . . .

"And I'll tell you the joy you do
Is simply what a blight is."

"And I'll tell you, and this is true,
You're worse than what uptight is."

"Then right away we will find out
What a holy fight is,
And both of us will fight and die
And never know what right is."

Who's to Blame?

Is this how you planned it, I don't understand it,
Please do not demand it of me.
A child will be crying, his dad will be dying.
It's these we were trying to free!
It's not my intention to violate convention,
If this is dissension—we'll see.
We came here to free them and not to puree them.
Oh, that's how you may see them?
Not me!
Well, I will now brand it, the work of a bandit,
And you will not hang it on me.
They say we are lying, you say they're defying,
Either way, Freedom's dying. I agree.
With us lies the blame, if we continue this game,
Our name will be Shame
Through the rest of our history.

In the Heat of Battle

In the heat of battle, we don't need ambivalence,
We would die at once if we failed to focus.
And our enemies would sweep over our fallen bodies
Devouring our land like the seven-year locus.

But in moments of peace, between our wars,
At least give reasoning a try.
Consider both sides of relevant issues—
Or all on both sides will die.

I'm Glad I'm No Hero

Lying in bed, listening to rain
That's pouring outside in the dark,
Wrapped in blankets, secured from the cold,
As sure as my name is Clark,
I'm glad I'm no hero, fighting great battles,
And damaged by each skirmish won.
Though people might praise me,
And heap on the honors,
If, by me, such fighting was done,
I'd be no more happy, and a lot more pain-full,
Living a life while half-dead.
So, I'll be without honors and unrecognized,
But happily all snug in my bed.

Another Brother

In our senseless civil war, brothers attacked one another,
And our nation, born in unity, was being torn asunder.
And only through patient forgiveness
Was hatred overridden.
And our nation of natural brothers
Overcame this terrible blunder.

We are now engaged in another war,
That's fought on foreign soil,
Some say in the name of liberty
Others in our lust for oil.
Whatever the flimsy reason,
Be it ignorance or foolish treason,
People still are dying before their appointed season.

And those we call our enemies kill us as we kill them,
And mercy has been forgotten,
And hatred is our national hymn.
Our civil war should have taught us
That when you slaughter your neighbors,
It's the sacred blood of brothers
That's dripping from your sabers.

And now our war's expanded,
As has our new disgrace,
Our nation has no borders, the worlds a smaller place.
Our history should have taught us,
You do not kill another—
The foe you name your enemy is just another brother.

In the Trenches

I'm rolling over red hills of Hell
And the flames are singeing my hair,
As I run in an ape-like crouch,
And my hot pit-fork is flailing
In the sulfurous fume filled air.
Then I tumble o'er the next pit railing,
Stabbing souls who are writhing there.

But they won't die, they just keeps on screaming.
When I stab them again, I don't care,
For I'm only here to torture,
And I have no pity to spare,
For these are the trenches of Hell,
That are dug by mortar and shell,
Where the souls of men are laid bare,

And I will not quit till my work is done
Until every man in these baleful pits
Has been tormented and loses his wits
And torn to shreds by my fork-like gun.
For this is how the battle is won—
And this work of the Devil has only begun.

Life on Mars?
After Edgar Rice Burroughs

There is no evidence of life on Mars today,
But hints of water say there might have been.
So had the atmosphere not gone astray,
Would Lords of Mars still rule,
As they might have done back then?

And if that's true, does life also exist
About some other stars?
And are there beings like us, pondering our lives,
Who have their own embattled Lords of Mars,
Who wonder whether sentient Earthen life
Somehow still survives?
And do they wish for Wiser Lives,
Who roam the distant-where,
Who'll guide us both beyond our foolish
And ever unending wars?

But even if they could,
Why then should those Old Wise Ones care?
Instead, they'd merely let us fall
And fade like the ancient War Lords on Mars.

I think those worrying lives must also do as we,
And rise above the hate that ruled on Mars,
And in our little time, until eternity,
Be wise enough, *ourselves,*
To end our own eternally endless wars.

Be Careful, The Body-Politic
Might Make You Sick

Conversations about war vary according to our personal or family experience with this historic preoccupation, but our feelings are also greatly affected by our current success in using war to carry out national agendas. Furthermore, our respect and support for those who are leading our war efforts is generally positive if we are winning and decidedly negative if we are losing.

As in sports, we flock to the stadium of a winning team, and only briefly watch the game on TV if our team is a loser. And, of course, it's the coach's fault—so fire the coach!

The really big Head Coach is our President, and in the next election he could be fired. But just remember, whomever we elect, we did the electing. This fallible human being, our leader, is only a little more responsible than we are.

Read on, but chew slowly.

Do We Really Want Another King George?

The democratic concept of check and balance
   Keeps one group from abusing its power.
Groups currently not holding power, say, "No, no,
   I'll remember this when I next have my hour."

So the group holding power only goes so far,
   So the little people struggling to survive,
As the pendulum swings from right to left,
   Needn't duck to at least stay alive.

Executive first has all the power,
   Until Congress rears up on its rump,
But then both of these powers have crow on their plates
   When the Supreme Court drops the last trump.

This struggle to balance the lust to use power
   Seems a waste of their time and too much of our money.
Why not give all the power to one of great wisdom?
   Then we'd all live our lives drinking milk laced with honey.

But that's what was tried throughout ages past,
   When kings told us God had made them so large
That all of us little folk must bow down and grovel—
   That's why we got rid of old crazy King George.

Our Lord, the President

The righteous among us at last got their way,
Jesus Christ ran for President and won.
Now, at last, there'd be Heaven on Earth,
(i.e. America), now *His* Presidency had finally begun.

The first hundred days were near ethereal,
The press and opposition kept their place,
The problems began, when Peter, The Adviser,
Told a lie, and was dismissed in disgrace.

Then a truly *big* problem occurred,
The Middle East burst into flame,
The President called for forgiveness—
They had only each other to blame.

But, though One God governed all,
Since Yahweh and Mohamed were one,
They still were destroying each other—
Claiming others were the ones who'd begun.

It was Congress' time to become righteous
How could the President be such a fool?
He should have heeded all us Americans
And not been an Israeli tool.

They knew, in their hearts, this was true,
The CEO's were beginning to boil,
Didn't He know our behemoth cars
Needed Iraqian Arabian oil?

Then next, the Nation felt terror,
And the People cried, "Let vengeance by thine!"
But the President said aggression was evil,
"I will love and not let anger be mine."

Then the Press sensed people weren't happy.
They implied that the President was weak,
And hinted that in the next term election—
Well, His ratings were well below peak.

Then the press to the right and the left
Came together to condemn His next vote.
Marriage was for *one* kind of people—
Those who came over on the Pilgrim's boat.

Then those people who secretly lusted
For the power of the President's throne
Began questioning the President's commitment.
Would He buckle when the nail bit the bone?

Now the President was sore brokenhearted,
In the West Wing, He knelt all alone,
Since Mary the Magdalene had left Him,
So He sank down, and none heard Him moan.

"My Father, why has't Thou forsaken
The Son whom You sent down to Earth?
Surely this hate that I've taken
Means I've more than proven My worth."

Then a brilliant white Phantom descended
And alighted near the President's ear.
"Oh my Son, You have filled Me with pride,
Without anger, You had only Your fear.

Continued . . .

"Yet You've honored Your office with caring,
But it's time that You left with Your hide,
And this time, You won't have to suffer—
You've *already* been crucified.

So the President announced He was leaving,
He'd resign at the end of His term,
Then all of American felt a shudder,
Beneath them, came the turn of The Worm.

And lo and behold, in the primaries,
Both parties put forth the same name,
And even the elders skipped the voting—
Acclamation was the name of the game.

And Father and Son, gazing down from above,
Lovingly, offered no blame,
For Americans finally got the leader we wanted—
Mister Satan was our new President's name.

The Power for Good or Bad

They say he's a good person, and that may well be true,
But if he tries to *impose* his enormous power to do
Only what *he* thinks we should do,
We should quickly raise the alarm,
Because even a man with the best of attentions
Can sometimes do terrible harm.

Mythical Methods of Mass Destruction

He was looking for weapons of mass destruction,
But it seems there were none to be found,
So he chose to use methods of myth-*math construction,*
Thereby proving myth-weapons were abound—
Zero times zero equals mythical destruction,
And thus thousands of weapons were found.

Hence, his up-coming November election
Wouldn't be ground in the really real ground.

I Am Your Leader

I am your leader, tell me what's true.
I know that you're frightened of what I might do.
If I just don't like what you're telling me
Will I banish, imprison, or decapitate you?

But the truth is, old comrade, we rose from the ranks,
And together we fought the right and left banks,
And now I'm your leader, and you are my aide,
So don't now let your courage and your loyalty fade.

While others bow down in fear of my power,
You must stand here by me in this terrible hour,
For if you don't tell me, in truth, who I am,
I'll be a mad leader, and not care a damn.

For all my subordinates will bow down in fear
And tell me only what I want to hear,
That I have great wisdom, and I'm always right,
And justified in using my God-given might,
And though many will parish before I am through,

Continued . . .

Isn't that is what great leaders are supposed to do?

Yes, I am your leader, but you are my friend,
So be a true friend and a friend to the end,
So when my reign's over and it's my time to go,
I'll be welcomed in Heaven and not sent below.

Our Leader's Children

Our leader has erred, and that behavior will haunt him
On next election day,
But the press is complaining that some of his children
Also have gone astray.
And one, in particular, is always behaving
No better than the worse kind of rebel.
But Jesus once told us only those without sins
Should cast out the very first stone—
But I'll question the integrity of anyone
Who picks up even the tiniest pebble today.

We Got it Wrong

We got it wrong, your government failed you,
And I apologize.
Thus spoke a courageous and truly honorable man
Before a government committee formed to separate lies
From painful truth, and no one knew
Our new reality better than
This man who would have been responsible
If things were done
That killed far more than he
Who caused our greatest tragedy—
The death of children is too great a price
No matter what was won.

And, yes, perhaps he did not rail enough—
　　　And thus the Devil wandered free.

　　But it was said that those who lead, and led,
　　　Were also honorable men.
　　They did what then was right,
　　Though time have told them wrong.
　　But is there anyone among us now
　　　Who would not do again
　　What honorable men have often done—
　　Waited cautiously, but just a bit too long?
　　Perhaps the lesson we must learn
　　Is do not judge the ones who led
　　Until we too must be responsible
　　For the acts that only we can take,
　　And when we do, though evil ones may die,
　　　The innocent will also then be dead.
But now at least let's honor one who told *his* truth—
And pity him those nights he now must lie awake.

Request or Command

　　Request, and I'll want to please.
　　Command, and I'll only comply.
　　Request, and I'll feel your respect
　　Command, and I'll question why.
　　Command, and I'll follow *your* lead.
　　Request, and *I'll* go to the fore.
　　Command, and I'll do what I'm told.
　　Request, and I'll do even more.

Continued . . .

Command is required for the weak.
Request assumes that I'm strong.
Command, and I'll only follow.
Request, and I'll know I'll belong
When I must lead our land
And request but seldom command.

Leading Your Sheep to Slaughter

We feed our dependent sheep,
So then we can harvest their wool.
We also feed on their meat.
Though sheep that are independent
Would also like to be full,
They avoid our fatal deceit.
*Our sh*eep have been bred to depend,
And free sheep are smart enough
To live without our attention,
So they usually survive in the rough.
It's a black sheep that leads the dullards
Down the slaughter-chutes to their deaths.
I wonder if those sheep that are slaughtered
Will cry out in their final breaths,
"Why did I follow that leader,
Was it worth all the food that he gave?
I also lead innocent children,
Who follow me into my grave."

So look about you, people, it is not a very big leap,
If you follow a self-serving leader,
You are being no more than sheep.

Yes, We Can Live With Gray

You *have* to know the truth of it,
You're not the same as I,
Your color's off, and mine is right—
There're other reasons why—
The language that you speak is not
The same my fathers taught,
The way you worship, *if you do,*
Is not the way you ought,
And I suspect that when you love,
If that's the thing you do,
You'll not produce a natural child
When what you've done is through,
And you're from there, and I'm from here,
We've always lived this way,
The world is either black or white,
We cannot live with gray.
And yet this world of right and left
Has led to years of pain,
And even now this way of hate
Has brought us war again.
I wonder if I placed my child
Beside a child of yours
If they would fight the way we do,
And blood flow down the sewers.
Or would they gently smile and coo
And touch each others hands,
And, by example, bind as one
Our not so different lands?

Continued . . .

111

So let us close our blinded eyes
And spread our minds today
And, with humility and love,
Let children lead the way.

Our Democratic Way

One and two and three,
You had better follow me!
Four and five and six,
Bring along your shooting sticks.
Sure as seven moves to eight,
There are people you should hate.
And as nine moves on to ten,
This will rope the voters in.

Ten descends until it's nine,
Shove those people back in line!
Quickly move along to eight,
They don't need to contemplate.
Seven says the blind must see,
Heaven is *our* property,
Six and five, and on to four—
We who have will get some more.

Three and two and one,
That is why our party won—
We knew how to count to ten,
And how to vote the party in.
And now that the election's won,
The other party's been undone,
And all the world is ours to win,
To make it all American.

Let's Try to Understand
How All of This Was Planned

The heavy part of the meal is over. Let's take a break before we decide if we want more, or if we want desert now or later. After all, we may have eaten a little too much.

Assuming we aren't too gastronomically uncomfortable, we might ease into a discussion of how we allowed ourselves to make so many mistakes in choosing our leaders and our national goals. Did we make those decisions with our greater goals in mind? And just what our greater goal anyway?

Well, knowing our greater goals also depends on how well we know ourselves. Just who are we, and how do we fit into the larger scheme of existence?

For a while, just eat nothing, or just pick at what's left on your plate while the conversation becomes somewhat philosophical.

The Illusion of Purpose and Why It's Important

As a child, I had purpose—
To eat to get bigger, and get bigger fast.
And when I studied, I had purpose,
To flatter my teachers for a passing grade,
When I married, I had purpose, to flatter my wife,
And make our relationship last.
When I worked, I had purpose, to flatter my boss
And thus get adequately paid.
When my children were born, I had wonderful purpose,
To keep them adored and alive.
When they passed adolescence, I had powerful purpose,
To hurriedly send them away.
And when I retired, my long delayed purpose?
Long leisure at first, and then to survive.

But now I'm near dying, what now is my purpose,
To lie here and pitifully pray?
When I think how life's purpose just led to more purpose,
Was there purpose in life after all?
Was it all just illusion, and the purpose non-being,
And all just a purposeless joke?
From the very beginning, should my purpose in being
Have been just avoiding this fall?

But just at this moment, I'm addressing these questions,
And a purposeful thought just awoke.
Of course, life has no purpose, accept what I give it,
So here's the connecting link,
Thinking and living are one in the same,
So *my purpose is continuing to think.*

Words

These are my words, they're all that I have,
And though they can burn, they also can salve.
Words are my tools, they help me to build.
And, yes, they are weapons, and they've also killed.

Words are revealers, they tell what I feel,
Words are deceivers, they hide what they steal.
These are my words, they're all I can be,
When all else is said, my words will be me.

Gurus

I've known a number of Gurus,
They're certainly impressive men.
In spite of their varied beliefs
They somehow entice people in.

Is it their aura of wisdom?
The doctrine they forcefully preach?
The promise of transformation
That's just beyond our reach?

Or is it our lack of faith
In what *we* thought we knew?
And we fail to say, "Gurus, get lost!
I know just as much as you."

Ether way, whatever we do,
We're all alone on that final day,
And the gurus' secret wisdom
Would probably just get in the way.

116

To Be or Not to Be
After Shakespeare and Descartes

You start with what you feel, or you don't start
At all. The mind does not exist unless
The senses first are stirred till they caress
Or stab the brain to make it do its part.

Though even then, the mind may hear no call.
Instead, it might just hover by and wait
To see if what you now will feel will make
You *be* a thought—or nothing else at all.

I've now described what I will call the "You,"
A thing that's greater than the parts that had
Occurred to leave you feeling good or bad,
That forces you to think what next to do—

To be or not to be what you create,
Your "Self" or just a non-existing state.

My Disappearing Act

They gathered all around me
And talked among themselves.
As loud as I was able, I shouted, "I am here!
And I can do a thing that no one else can do.
I can disappear!"

Continued . . .

I spoke about myself, and all that I had done.
I listed all the folks who knew of me.
I looked into their eyes, and none looked back at me,
Because I wasn't there for anyone to see.

I'd done one magic act, but I would do far more,
For then I did a greater trick than ever done before,
I was not there again *because I'd never been*
And might as well not ever be again.

I was the great magician, who was, but was not there.
The only trick I could not do, when all the people stare
And look right through my lonely soul—
Is shout, *I do not care!*
That's why I am not here. That's why I disappear.

Make Haste

Brisk wind upon my face, make haste,
Lead me to that other place.
Where all my doubts and all my fears
Will flit away without a trace.
And there, the sun is warm, and will not burn,
And cooling streams will welcome me at every turn,
And for a time, there'll be no time, and no one there but me.
And when I do return, the one whom you will see
Will bring back from that other place another face
That shows a warmer heart, a cooler mind
Than those I left behind
When last I left this painful place.
Make haste!

Sing Your Own Song

Strolling down the street one day
I passed a man who sang a song.
I cringed to hear the awful way
He sang. It couldn't be more wrong!

But when I came right up to him,
And looked upon his face,
I saw a smile. He was not grim.
My cringe was out of place.

I learned this lesson on that day,
My judgment matters not,
Let others sing their own darn way,
Who says *my* song's so hot?

We Must Sail Together

He slowly walks among us, but he's no longer here.
That which made his center is now no longer there.
He's like an empty shell. When put up to the ear,
There is no whispered ocean, there's only silent air.

Perhaps he's on that ocean, seeking what he's lost,
A purpose for existing, a reason he should care.
But all he feels is sadness, a heart that's tempest tossed,
But even that is fading. It goes, he knows not where.

We too must sail that ocean, that emptiness inside,
When that which gave us purpose is then no longer dear.
Or might we sail together, before the final tide,
And be not empty shells while we're remaining here?

I'm Walking in the Wintry Woods

I'm walking in the wintry woods
When trees have lost their autumn leaves,
And I can see beyond their barren trunks
And feel a bracing breeze,
And bundled in my warmest clothes,
The chill just strokes my face,
And though I've yet a way to go,
This is my chosen walking place.

But now I take a trail that I have never used,
That's just around the bend.
Then next, I cut across a hill to find a faster way
To reach my journey's end.
But then I come upon a bog and unfamiliar trees.
I try, but can't recall
This boulder here, this fallen log—
In fact, I don't remember ever being here at all.

I peer into the sky to seek the west,
And all I see is mist that hides the sun.
The *ghost* of hidden east is all I know,
And now the winter's darkness has begun.

The bracing breeze becomes a biting wind,
And clothes I wear are far too thin.
My only thought is, stay alive
Until I find the missing trail again.

I stumble on, my hope is fading fast,
And soon I fear my feeble legs will fail,
Then in the dark, I trip upon a log,
And fall, face-first upon the bless-ed trail.

A window light then parts the night,
And I can sense the welcomed warmth of home.

I've learned my lesson, this I truly swear,
If in the winter woods I ever choose to roam,
I'll walk along a way I *know* is there.
Though walking in the woods may be a lark,
In woods *or life*,
If I intend to find my way, I will not leave the trail
When walking in the winter's dark.

Get-Through-able

Never mind the possible, the probable is more doable.
Start out doing, step-by-step,
The tiny steps along the way,
And eventually the larger step will be get-through-able.
And, who knows, maybe some great day,
The possible, or even the impossible,
Will also be come-true-able.

Why Do We Go to the Movies?

Why do we go to the movies?
It takes too much money and time.
We now pay ten dollars or more.
In my childhood it cost just a dime.
So why not the lending library,
Where we can borrow a low cost book?
Because that requires mental effort,
And in movies you just sit back and look.

Continued . . .

And why should we read, or why should be look,
What do these efforts provide?
What's wrong with the world that we live in,
And from what are we seeking to hide?
Have our own lives become too overwhelming
Or maybe just boring or dull,
And life on the screen has more meaning,
Since nothing takes place in our skull?

Are the lives that we live in the movies
More real than the real lives we live?
And we give all our love in the movies
Because in real life we have no love to give?
The answer to all of these questions,
And the only way we will ever win,
Is to find more meaning in day-to-day living
And then risking our own living again.

Not 'Neath the Old Muddy River

New Orleans, New Orleans,
You city of easy sin,
And wind has brought new reality,
And your easy will not come again.

Let us grieve for your dead *and* your living,
And this City of Saints as well,
Katrina, the Rage from the South,
Leaves New Orleans a long-living Hell.

There will be a time for thanksgiving,
And prayers for return of the past,
But a city that lives 'neath a river
Is a city that cannot last.

It is time for those who have substance,
Who survived the storm without pain,
To counsel the suffering thousands,
That the water will return again.

Let us give till we too are hurting,
To rebuild without being insane,
Yea, not 'neath the old muddy river
Where the water will destroy you again.

Childhood's End in New Orleans

As a child, I lived in New Orleans,
Roberts Street, Jenna Street, Fontainebleau Drive.
Beneath the floods from Lake Pontchartrain,
Is there anything still left alive?

The Catholic schools I attended,
The churches where communion was given,
The Sisters who paddled my palms
So my few childish sins would be shriven.

What horrifies me most is the loss of my friends.
And that prettiest girl that I knew?
Did she linger too long in New Orleans,
And the waters have buried her too?

I Curse you, Katrina, and call you a killer,
You murdered my past with your wind.
Now my heart is lost in your flooding,
And my childhood has come to an end.

Some Personal Comparisons

By making comparisons you'll reveal who you are,
But be sure what you actually say,
For a metaphor that may seem to be right
May be seen in a less pleasant way.

Like:
I'm as deep as a well—but my bottom's exposed when the
sun is on high,
And a well sometimes is shallow,
And a well may also run dry.

Or:
I'm as wise an owl—except throughout the day
When this wise old owl has fallen asleep and hasn't a thing to say.

I was as bright a penny—but now I'm just rusty and old.
So never mind being copper,
I'd rather be untarnishable gold.

I'm as dead as a doornail—but that's not always true,
A doornail feels very lively when it's puncturing my shoe.

I'm as old as the hills—yet hear this hill sing,
Because I know I sound youthful
When I'm coated with Spring.

I'm as deep as the ocean, and that means that I'm wise,
But down deep in the ocean, a wise man dies.

I'm as bright as a firefly—but my light will go dead,
If I'm lit up too late and I don't get to bed.

I'm as black as a coal—but a coal can be lit.
So take care where you're walking and don't walk on it.

I'm as meek as a mouse—but a mouse has sharp teeth,
And when pinned on his back, it bits from beneath.

I'm as white as a lily, and I spout like a spigot.
I think I know right, but I'm sometimes a bigot.

I'm as fit a fiddle, because I eat like a bird.
Now I'm light as a feather, but that's getting absurd.

I'm as brave as a lion—but as soft as a pillow
When my lioness starts purring or weeps like a willow.

I'm remote like the mountains, and as cold as I'm wise,
But the weeping of children brings tears to my eyes.

I am crafty, not craven. I'm a wolf, not a fox.
But my heart's all a flutter when I touch Goldilocks.

I'm as green as a garden that's sprouting in spring,
But as barren as winter when *your* ice does its thing.

I'm as bright as the leaves that flame in the fall,
But as dark as a dungeon in dread Dracula's hall.

I'm as warm a the wind that flows through a fire
Or as cold as a heart that's lost all desire.

I'm as fast as a flea that flits through the air,
And as tough as the tick that's stuck in my hair.

Continued . . .

125

I'm as wild as the wind, or as soft as a breeze,
It depends on which woman now sits on my knees.

I'm as glittery as gold, or as precious as pearls,
But my wealth will be worthless
If it's spent it just on girls.

I'm as high as the Heavens and as deep as the sea,
And as warm as the south wind
When you're sleeping with me.

I'm either as high as an elephant's eye,
Or as low as a worm that squirms under earth,
But I can stand tall, if I give life my all—
I was only a worm nine month before birth.

I'm a bird that came from an egg
That lay in the nest too long,
I never learned how to fly,
And my feathers will never get dry,
And I only know how to sing a pitifully half-learned song.

My cream may rise to the top—
But churn it and it turns to butter,
But either will sours after too many hours,
And a poor little calf has but mom's empty udder.

Continued . . .

So these sayings may say who I am,
And sometimes who I am not,
And sometimes I'm right on target,
And others nowhere near the spot.

But I am an arrow, released from the bow,
To go wherever I'll go.
And when I have fallen finally to earth,
There's one thing that you must know,
Either I pierced through the truth, or missed by a mile,
Or barely missed it by a sliver,
But for a while I was free as an arrow,
And I did not remain in the quiver.

The Door Closed

The door closed, *but no one entered the room,*
And all was quite as though I dwelled
In an otherwise empty tomb.
Was there a ghost who had come to torture me?
And if I dared to blink my eyes,
What horrors would I suddenly see?

So, eyes still closed, I crept to reach
That silently haunted door.
There had to be even more,
I had to see, though blind of eye,
What might still be waiting out there,
But all I felt was the all-frigid air,
And all I heard were some silent cries—
Then I could see, through still closed eyes,
What any fool should realize,
That it's only fear that remains
When a lifetime of courage dies.

Truths from Pictures and Words

Psychologists display their pictures
　　Before their patients' eyes,
And what the patients say they see
　　Reveals their truths or lies,
The hopes and fears they harbor
　　And hide within the mind.
The pictures are not truth—
　　That, only patients find.

The poet spreads his words instead,
　　To touch the readers' ear,
And what the readers hear
　　May surface hope or fear.
The poet's words are maps,
　　And truths there one may find,
But greater truths may yet be born
　　Within the readers' mind.

So poets and doctors, do your best
　　To help your people see
What those who have the courage,
　　And then the will to be,
Will find within themselves
　　What you yourselves must find—
All truth that's worth the knowing is found within the mind.

Our Lust for Certainty

Our lust for certainty can lead to absurdity,
So when someone says that he knows what is true
We give up our freedom to think,
And do what he tells us to do,
And swallow answers that will turn out to be.
So utterly illogical we will slide to the brink
Of what is certainly insanity.

Are the planets in charge of our destiny?
Can cards determine our ultimate fate?
Would we rather believe in a fantasy future
Just because we're too fearful to wait?

The fault, I suspect, is our science
It's destroyed our old-time religion
On which we had total reliance,
And now *we* must make each decision.

But we fear that the choices we make
Will lead to a lifetime of pain.
Who will help us avoid the mistake
We must never make again?

Never mind, let's not *think* about it.
That is how our troubles began.
Logic? We can do without it.
And if, what's it called, hits the fan,
That's alright, we'll make that our heavenly plan.

Dreams, Then and Now

These were the dreams of childhood,
The dreams from which latter dreams grow,
A castle within sargasso seaweed,
And a horse that flies me wherever I go,

Sunsets that are ever golden,
Oceans that are always blue,
Sages who rule through their wisdom,
Heroes who are always true,

A mansion that reaches the heavens
With a golden celestials door
That opens to admit all the nobles
And the equally noble poor,

Preachers who offer here-after
But help with my everyday fears,
Teachers who teach math and reading
But comfort when I break into tears.

Yes, these were dreams of my childhood,
But in moving through life's later stages,
I have dreams that demand greater wisdom
Even more so than those mythical sages.

I dream of a god up in Heaven
Who created eternity,
Who now leaves all subsequent choices
To fallible humans like me.

The Atheist

Just because you think you're smart,
Don't take away another's religion.
When each of you comes to the end,
Will *you* have time for *your* decision?

If how he's prayed will ease his way,
This thought might have arisen.
If yet you haven't thought it through,
Ask how *you* will meet that day
If your dumb soul must then be shriven?

So that's what's wrong with being smart
You're never smart enough,
And dying with no answers known
Has got to be damn tough.

Though Lies May Make You Happy

Though lies may make you happy,
Do not be deceived
The truth, though often painful,
Must always be believed.

I told myself a falsehood
And made myself believe
That it would make me happy
Now all I do is grieve.

And so I've gained this wisdom,
If choice should come again
I will not choose dumb-happy,
I'll choose instead some pain.

My Seven Sins

At my life's end
My soul won't bend
I'll ride the wind
And head for Heaven.

And I'll declare
To Him up there
My souls laid bare—
Presenting seven.

Yes, seven sins
My soul defends
To make amends—
Since I'm sin laden.

The first was love,
Not for the Dove
That dwells above
But for a maiden.

The next was spite
That came the night
When died delight
And love departed.

The third was hate.
I did berate
My loving mate
And was mean-hearted.

Continued . . .

The forth was fear
I'd settled here
Upon my Dear—
I did abuse her.

The fifth was fright
That she was right
That from our fight
I now would loose her.

The sixth was brawn
I used that dawn
That sent her on
To early Heaven.

So here I stand
My own death planned
By my own hand.
That's number seven.

And now I know
Where I must go,
It's down below
Not into Heaven.

So heed my call,
You *too* shall fall
If you don't stall
The deadly seven!

Crumbing Monument
After Shelley

I'll leave no crumbling monument out on the desert sand,
Proclaiming I had been much more than merely mortal man.
My only contribution, the only thing I'd done,
Was pass along a part of me because I had a son.

Then like that ancient ruler,
Who thought we'd know his name,
I hope the sons who follow me, would someday do the same.
And through their sons-of-sons, I'll have my share of fame,
If even one or more of them will know my given name.

When we're alive, the world is ours, and that's our time to be,
But if *you* ask for more than this, to live through history,
And fame throughout eternity is what you've always planned,
You'll also find your fame is buried here
Beneath the desert sand.

Don't Expect to Have it All

If you expect to have it all, think again.
Living means compensating.
If this makes you're despondent,
Put this under your bonnet
And wisely think upon it,
Don't waste time overrating
Having it all—That's no way to win.

The wisest way to "have it all," hear again,
Living means compensating!
Take what comes to you each day.
Though it's bad, do not dismay,
Start again another day.
It might be scintillating,
And though not all, better than it might have been.

Ancient Idols are Lost

From myths, there was Prometheus,
From the Republic, Cincinnatus—
Noble beings once admired by all.
What has become of our models,
What has caused this precipitous fall?
Why do we idolize a rock star,
A child molester looking like a beauty queen?
Rather than honoring virtue,
We elevate the grossly obscene.
Why do we bow to such icons,
Why have we sunk so low,
Encouraging our children to emulate
Those we should have sent down below?
The answer must be in ourselves,
In our sloth, we're too lazy to strive.
Our machines do all the work that we need.
Minimal effort will keep us alive,
So aspiring to something more noble
Makes us face that we just lack the will,
So we set our wimp-like sights
Beneath the very bottom of the smallest hill.
Prometheus, Cincinnatus, and others,
Who inspired us in times gone by,

Continued . . .

Look down from your lofty perch
And tell us we're living a lie,
That if we just get off our bottoms,
We too could ascend to the sky.

Moon Knowledge

It well may be that nothing's new under the sun—
But there's always the moon.
In the minds of men, in the dark of night,
Comes to light many a marvelous and divergent tune.

As the dreams explore what's unknown before,
What puzzles in day may find some new way
To bring to the sun what the moon may have won
Till finally from dreaming, what's new finds the day.

Dreaming of Winds

I love to hear the breezes blow outside my window pane,
Whether through a balmy sky or in the pouring rain,
A gentle breeze, a howling wind, they all will call to me,
"Desert your bed, come join with us,
You too can wander free."
But with a sigh, I turn them down, as happy as they seem,
The winds are what I dream about, my bed is *where* is dream.
So, after all, I guess my bed is where I'd rather be.

My Dreams

My dreams may taunt or encourage me,
Inspire me or discourage me,
Or agonize, infuriate, scintillate
Tranquilize, fascinate, facilitate,
Or seem like second sight,
Mystify, clarify, or terrify
And fill my nights with fright,
But most of all, most certainly,
They get me through the night.

You Don't Define the World

Though it may seem that way,
You don't define the world.
But I'm not surprised, I have to say
Others may think as you.
But neither you, nor I, nor they
May define the world, all that's already been unfurled.
Either The Master of All, or the collective we,
Has and will define what the world may be.
And as for me,
The collective we will do.

Is This Important?

There is a fountain,
Perhaps you've seen it when you traveled out to sea.
It's from a mountain, the rises from the ocean floor.
You only see it when you sink beneath the waves.
And once you've seen it, you will never see it more.
Is this important?
Perhaps it is—to no one else but me.

137

There was a brother,
Perhaps you heard what he had always tried to be.
But he was other than the person
Who could do what needed done,
And so when time ran out on him,
He had fallen to his knees,
And the race that he was running,
Someone else had always won.
Is this important?
Perhaps it is—to no one else but me.

There is a question,
Perhaps you've asked yourself,
"What could the answer be?"
Here's a suggestion,
Perhaps the only place you'll ever find
The answer that you missed
When you were down beneath the sea
Is somewhere deep within an altered state of mind.
Is this important?
Perhaps it is—to no one else but me.

One final question,
Perhaps you've asked it
But only when you needed company.
But the people whom you asked
Just let your question pass,
For they all feared the answer
That you sought to know,
And so they buried *all* your questions under grass.
Is this important?
Perhaps it is—to no one else but me.

Sprite in My Mind

Oh what will you find,
Wise sprite of my mind,
When you fly so high
You transfix the sky
And in your far flight
You then banish the night?
And what would I do
If I could conspire
To travel with you
And climb even higher?

And what would I see
Looking down on the world,
The Eden not vanished,
With its beauties unfurled—
The mountains, the valleys
The forests, the sea
All Heaven on Earth
Enrapturing me?

Then what would I do
But fly even higher
And reach for the sun
And bask in its fire.
Though there in its bosom
My life would expire,
There'd be no sadness
They'd be no grief,

Continued . . .

There'd be only gladness
In my certain belief,
As I burned in the sun,
That nothing could match
What I'd already done.

But what should I do,
I am still here below?
If I can't travel up
Where else should I go?

I'll seek that sprite
That resides in my mind
And sink even deeper,
And if I'm not blind,
I know I will find
What I saw up there
When I banished the night.
For, after all, all Heaven
Was born from a sprite
That only exists in my mind.

Cave of Night

Why do I fear you, Cave of Night?
Why do I fear the loss of light?
Aren't you a roof that will shelter me
From burning sun and freezing snow?
So, I won't hesitate, within I'll go,
And in time, my courage will show
Beyond the cave is eternity.

Castles in My Mind

Alas, our house has burned down,
All of the way to the ground,
And nothing that we cherished, anywhere can be found.
And, yes, I was crying—a great part of me was dying—
And though we dug in the ashes,
Nothing of valuable had been left behind.
So now I'm just grateful—
For those castles that I build in my mind.

What Else Am I?

Having been born, I have no doubt
I'm a male, and my mother had a lover.
But what else am I—a father, a son,
A nephew, a grandpa, or even a brother?
Well, there're only two things that I'm sure about,
I'm not the Holy Ghost,
And I'm not His Holy Mother.

Dream With Care

The things you saw while dreaming
Were really never there,
And now as you lie awake,
No matter how hard you stare,
You'll see but empty air.
So have your pleasant dreaming
But then, for Heaven's sake,
No matter how nice it's seeming,
Don't dream while you're awake.

Revelation

Come alive, little one, where have you been?
It seems I haven't seen you before.
I knew both your parents, and they were just fine,
But I think you'll become even more.

I remember an infant, somewhere back then,
Who was almost as happy as you.
But I guess I was careless, for that happy young child
Lived in great pain before he was through.

So here's my last chance, I am letting you loose,
And I hope before you are done,
You'll have finished the task that I set for you both,
And Revelation will then have begun.

Awe

When time is empty and I wonder why I live,
I read, or watch the stars, or ponder night.
And when these efforts give all that they will give
And reasons sought have yet to fill my sight,

A thought has come I've never known before,
And with that thought a feeling has arrived,
Like sunlight beaming through an opened door,
Or sparkling seas through which my soul has dived.

It is a wonder, it is amazement filled with glee,
It is a warmth that drive away the inner cold,
A weight removed that sets my spirit free,
A childlike hope that never will grow old.

Then there's the mind that was an empty slate,
That infant mind that bore no hint of art,
That fills with thoughts to finally create
A work of art to overwhelm the heart.

And then I think what I have thought before,
Amazement that this creature, who is less than naught
Who now is me, and nothing more,
Could conjure up so feelingful a thought.

And awe is what I name what I have come to feel
And marvel that this empty life could give
A reason that's not metaphor, but real—
To feel such awe is why I chose to live.

The World of Keening Words

The wind was bearing words I did not recognize,
They tantalized because I only *felt* their meaning.
They came from other worlds and other skies
Where sad and frightened fowls were keening.
And then the wind became a mournful breeze,
Until the words were barely whispers,
And yet it seemed that someone begged, "Oh Please,
Oh Please, I need attentive listeners!"

So when the breezes finally died away,
I did my best to hear the keening birds
And understand what they had tried to say.
Until at last, I recognized the words
I thought had come from frightened birds
Were coming from another place.
There was no world of keening words—
Except the world behind my face.

Continued . . .

Perhaps, I'd better listen now,
And this time listen well,
Perhaps the words will tell me how
To break the wind-born spell,
So if the words within are words of fear,
I won't again be haunted by the wind.
I'll hear the words *I choose* to hear
And know the keening wind as friend.

This Too Shall Pass

The wisest of men was asked,
"Why should I continue to live
Now that my loved one has left me,
And I gave all the love I could give?'
And he replied, "This too shall pass."

The wisest of men was asked,
"Why should I endure such pain
When those I've raised destroy themselves,
Over and over again?
And he replied, "This too shall pass."

The wisest of men was asked,
"Why must I cringe and cower
When those I trusted to rule,
Deceive and abuse their power?"
And he replied, "This too shall pass."

The wisest of men was asked,
Why God allows the Earth to spin
When those to whom He gave the Earth
Continue to live in sin?
And he replied, "This too shall pass."

The wisest of men was asked,
"Why did the universe evolve,
To only end in misery,
Which my mind cannot resolve?"
And he replied, "This too shall pass."

The wisest of men was asked,
"Why should I care what I've heard
When all the *wisdom* you've spoken
Seems trite or merely absurd?"
And he replied, "This too shall pass."

The wisest of men was asked,
Why this was all he would say,
That life will go on if I'll but endure
Another unending day.
And he replied, "I've one more thing to say.
When life's an empty glass—
Since you have drunk it all—*I too shall pass.*"

And then I knew at last
That He who filled the empty glass
Was He who said to me, "This too shall pass."

Your Time in Eternity

Though I still have short-run time,
The long-run time is running out.
So I've time to do a mass of things,
But there can be no doubt
That the Keeper-of-Time is calling time on me
And his final bell will sound.
So I am doing a lot, and rapidly,
So much that I sometimes astound
Those younger folks who don't understand
What time is all about:

Get done in time what can be done,
This time is all they'll be
Of your little moment in time
In all of eternity.

Why Learn to Read?

We are forcing our children to read.
Why? Where does it lead?
Before, they were innocent.
Now, their learning has sent them
Over the brink to slowly sink
Into the mired down adult world
Where innocence has lost its link
With all that came before.

And what was lost?
That emptiness that knew no fear
Of what would come
When once again our learning brains
Return to numb.

Yet, no doubt it's better
That we learn to read.
That pregnant seed
Will blossom forth and fill our living days
With knowledge of the ways
We'll need to be
To live in full our too few days—
Before returning to that all eternal infancy
That has no need to read.

Take Heed!

To lead or not to lead?
There is no question.
If you are appointed,
And choose not to lead,
Those who follow you
Will make you bleed.

Take heed!

What's Life Worth
Without the Earth That Gave us Birth

A little of our over-eating has been digested, and we're feeling pleasantly satiated, and it occurs to us that we should be grateful for all the bounty we've received. The discussion renews with the realization that all our food, now-a-days, is dependent on our modern technology—and that brings with it some undesirable side effects.

Individually, we are not the only ones affected by our technological onslaught, the environment in general is disturbed. Still, at a deeper level, we are grateful for the natural environment that remains, and concern for that leads to a discussion of the Earth and our place on it. Who knows, maybe we should return to our primitive beginnings—before we are *forced* to descend to the primitive because our greed is demanding too much from the Earth.

Our New Masters

Kings and emperors of old had servants and slaves
To do their laborious chores.
They cleaned their castles, washed their linens,
Swept out dog-leavings from straw-laden floors,
Spent months in planting and harvesting fields,
And hours preparing sometimes primitive meals,
And even wet-nursed their children,
And answered their bawling late-night appeals.
Of course, their caring was not without cost,
Slaves and servants had to be housed and fed.
When the food ran out, the slaves rebelled,
And the kings either fled—or were dead.

But now those papered,
Though unfortunate rulers,
Are nowhere around to be found,
And we, former servants and slaves,
Are now on top of the mound.
And nowadays we are living like kings,
And our servants are electrons that live in machines,
And we expect from *our* minions even finer services
Than did earlier Kings and their queens.

But there's still a risk that we're taking
In depending on this electronic hoard.
They may be even more dangerous than electronic slaves,
And a risk too great to afford.
One day our electronic minions
Could put our soft necks to the sword
And become our electronic masters—
As we spend all of our waking-time
Repairing the machines that keep us captive
So we don't die in our over-pampered prime.

I Was Born in an Age of Words

I was born a little before
This amazing electronic age,
In which instant gratification,
Through continual minification,
Is the impetus of our economy
And the ever increasing rage.

So I must beg my all-clever son,
Before my own work's begun,
To explain how to use my cellular phone
And how my computer works,
With all of its frustrating quirks,
Or my own work will never be done.

But I was born in an age of words,
Where I learned to employ these tools
To understand rare geniuses,
And sometimes even cleverer fools,
To help them live with each other
Through carefully worded rules.

But I think when all's said and done,
Our electrons are here to stay,
And they'll do even more everyday
In their clever electronic way,
But it's words with their greater complexity
That are now and always will be
What will help us word-users see it through
And somehow survive and live on
Even if our amazing electronic gadgets are gone.

Cars on Mars

Sending all of our cars to Mars
Certainly sounds propitious,
So then the air back on the Earth
Would smell again, delicious.
But this would be seditious,
And all of our auto makers
Would force the fools who'd planed this plan
To visit undertakers.

Instead, they'd fly their cars back here
Ignoring their putrid pollution,
Until our Earthen seas are becoming
A toxic chemical solution.
Then, because of our cars—*And all of our wars*—
There'd be no more Earthen sea,
And all of the Earth would be desolate
As desolate could ever be—
And no where near as happy
As the happily un-polluted Mars.

Let's Still Smell the Flowers

Flowers were once what we cherished.
We grew them and arranged them as art.
Although they were ephemeral, and perished,
For a while they gladdened the heart.

But now an electronic machine
Is displayed in each room in the house.
What was once hidden as obscene
Is *the art* that we give to our spouse.

Continued . . .

Although they are plastic, and usually dead,
Their colors are sometimes so bright
That they rival our gay flowerbed,
And they also light up at night.

We may appreciate our electronic servers,
When they sometimes behave as they should,
But we don't have to be art-knowing observers
To know that flowers would smell twice as good.

Cardboard Castles

Over-large cardboard boxes make wonderful castles
For children's imaginary play.
They crawl in and out, and they laugh and they shout
As they dwell there in joy through the day.

But similar boxes make pitiful castles
If you have nowhere else you can sleep.
As you lie all alone, often chilled to the bone,
You don't laugh, you don't shout, you just weep.

A Mental Chameleon

I am a mental chameleon,
I can change opinions as rapidly
And as often as needed to thrive.
No opinion is sacred to me. I only worship one
As long as it keeps me alive.
So I guess I'm almost as smart as lizards,
And they've been on Earth since forever—
And they still survive.

Dandelions

Why are you so maligned,
You golden headed herb?
You're beautiful and edible,
So why must we disturb
The Earth's eternal plan
That brings you forth each spring
To offer love as foods,
Your tender leaves for salads,
And herbal teas for moods?
And even when your head-dress
Becomes a gossamer white,
Our children pick those halos
And blow them off into flight.

So why are we so unkind?
You die, but we don't care.
If fact, we would be happy
If you were never even there.

And if you dare to linger,
An herbicide's your fate.
The love you tried to give us
Returns to you as hate.

But you're too common for us,
We must maintain our class.
In neighborhoods we live in
The lawns must all be grass.

Continued . . .

But now I've told your story,
I know it's love you bring.
So hear me, haughty neighbors,
We've done a foolish thing—

Onto your cruel opinions,
I will no longer cling.
So golden one, don't worry
I'll love you come the spring

Carry Me Back to Old Virginia

Carry me back to our home in Virginia,
Back among the poplar, the oak, and maple trees.
Climbing up those steep hills is certain to re-skinny-ya,
But never mind, our sweating brows
Will be drying in the gentle mountain breeze.

But mostly it's serenity that will always a-winy-ya
And bring us back home on our gladly grateful knees.
I guess we're bound to die in old Virginia—
With assistance from our auto-wrecking deer
And our painful Lyme disease.

God Shouldn't Own a Tree

If you plant a sapling, and nurture it when it's small,
It'll belong to you—but only till it's tall.
It's like your child, as it grows, you set it free—
Neither you nor God should ever own a tree.

Kudzu Plants Cover All

Along some Southern highways, kudzu plants cover all,
And all of these verdant vines drape the landscape like a pall
And devastate the trees with miles of carpeting death—
And yet their sculptured beauty,
Will take away your breath.
Each bend along the highway presents celestial themes
That only could have happened
In the Sistine painter's dreams.

And yet beneath this beauty, a death is underway,
And trees that would be forests will never see the day.
For what might seem like beauty may have another need,
And what we wish to cherish has just become its feed.

So as we drive *life's* highways, it's best we all take care,
To seek beneath the surface and find what might be there,
And cure our fearful blindness
And see what should have been—
To open up our thinking and let the sunlight in.

Climbing Up Simonside[*]

I'm climbing up old Simonside as dusk is easing in,
For this is where my forebears climbed,
And now I climb again.
I won't come down till meeting those men who led to me.
They did their duty for their kin, and now I will do mine,
"Fathers from my ancient past, I give my thanks to thee,
So those who follow after me will make the future thine."

[*]A boulder strewn ridge, in Northumbria, where cairns mark
the passage of pre-English ancestors.

What Does It Take to be Human?

What does it mean to be human,
No longer merely a beast
That arose from the primeval swamp
From a bonding of primitive yeast?
What happened in gray nether regions
Of an early mammalian brain
When the loss of instinctual control
Was our primitive consciousness' gain,
When more than instincts would determine
The decisions we humans would make,
To build a home in a cavern
Or on stilts on a cold mountain lake,
To gather the tribal members
And, later, each primitive band,
To travel to distant horizons
To cultivate oceans of land?
What does it mean to be humans
Who create and then war as nations
Then teeter on the brink of destruction
Of all of our human creations?
What will it take to remain human
When the beasts still rule from within
And drive us to mindless behaviors
That could force us to start over again?

Perhaps it will mean evolution
Must drive us to seek and to find
The combining of all of humanity
Into only one human mind.

The Bulbs of Perennial Love

Perennial flowers, the children of bulbs,
Arise in the early spring.
Iris, daffodils, and tulips awake,
And the winter-weary sing.
Previous owners had buried these bulbs,
People with lives of their own,
Prepared all these beds, planted there bulbs,
And left them to grow all alone.
Where are these planters of other days?
Have their lives grown
As well as their flowers?
Did they weather their winters,
And reap their benefits
From summer sunshine and showers?
Whoever they were and wherever they are,
I hope there're as happy as I,
Who benefits from their labors of love,
From these plants that will never die.
This promise I give, for as long as I live,
I'll continue the work you've begun,
And someday another will see our bright flowers
And wonder by whose hands this was done.

What Earth Has Begun

Bromeliads are cups filled with water,
When they're dry they sip from themselves.
Whereas, toadstools are made for the rain,
Since their tops are umbrellas for elves.

Continued . . .

Roses are virtuous ladies,
Their thorns are protection from sin.
The Venus flytrap is the Devil
Who beckons all us sinner in.

Dandelions are bright yellow carpets,
Protecting soft earthen floors.
Sea oats are wardens of beaches
Guarding windblown sand on the shores.

Mushrooms are miners of midnight
Unearthing dawn's white fairy rings.
Forget-me-nots are reminders
Of otherwise forgotten things.

Bright painted leaves are announcing
That winter is soon on its way.
And mistletoe is the promise
That those winter chills will not stay.

Buttercups are banquets for bees
That are shared with the queen of each hive.
Lichen is a luncheon in winter
Keeping the caribou alive.

Ivy's a daredevil climber
That strives for the very best view.
Lilies are sermons at Easter
Proclaiming that life springs anew.

Seeds are the Earth's buried treasures
That will purchase new life in the spring.
Buds are the babies of parents
Who did Mother Nature's thing.

All of these children of Nature
Will grow in the love of the sun,
And we are but *one* among many—
Let's not end what the Earth has begun!

Drink Milk or Water

Coffee and Coke won't cause you to choke,
But neither will make you serene.
And all of that sugar they put in a Coke
Will never help you grow very lean.

So you would be smarter to drink milk , or just water,
And then when your frame hits the scene,
You'll be calm as a statue, but lean
As a body that looks and acts like a teen.

Is There Hope Beyond the End?

I stared into the sky and saw the end—
Beyond the final star there was no light,
As suns descended into endless night,
Where galaxies would weep and never mend.
Then stars disbursed to meet their lonely fate,
And warmth that gave us life had died as well,
And human brains, and every single cell,
Collapsed again to one atomic state.

But that forlorn and dreadful time is then,
And this is now. While there's still ample light,
Should we despair and curse the coming night
And weep for all the good that might have been,
Or hope there's yet a place where we'll belong,
So that the end we thought we saw was wrong?

Painting the Seasons

With hot breath sighing, summer greenery is dying,
And autumn's begun bronzing the land.
As the crystalline phantom of winter waits quietly
To paint all the land with its silvering hand.

Though winter be weary, dark days and dreary,
With nights so much longer than days,
And warmth of the summer, and glory of autumn,
Seem vanished forever in memory's haze,

You don't hear me sighing, and forget about dying,
Nor am I fearing what winter will bring.
For I'm painting my memory in the blossoming colors
That are spread on the palette of spring.

I'll have to Move on Again

They're building houses around me.
I'll have to move on again.
Somewhere deep in the forest,
Surrounded by primitive men.

My soul was born in the woodlands,
And that's where I now long to be,
Only in living beyond people,
Am I allowed to be free.

So off I will go in the morning,
Seeking to find that new place
Where having no houses around me
Will vanished the whole human race.

And if you also would follow,
Come with me, and hurry, make haste!
Like those of my brothers, the natives,
My footprints can never be traced.

Oh What Vanity

We built our little hovels.
Later, structures to challenge the sky,
Temples, cathedrals, and palaces,
We were certain would never die.

Then came a laughing breeze
That quietly twisted and swirled
And soaked up heat from the ocean
And began to cover the world.

We call it names to control it,
Like Andrew, Frances, or Elaine,
But *it* knew in its malevolent heart
Its true name was Hurricane!

Oh what vanity, that tiny mortals,
Infinitesimal spawn of the Earth,
Believed we could challenge our Mother,
When giants were hers to give birth.

But, foolish and vain we may be,
We wrench ourselves from our sorrow
And build again from the rubble
And dream of a better tomorrow.

Though foolish and vain we remain
Next time, our dreams will not fail,
Come hurricane, earthquake, or whatever —
For now, till whenever, we'll prevail!

Oh, How Vicious Life is

Oh, how vicious Life is, for this monster to survive,
Other lower forms of life no longer are alive.
Who arranged these atoms, that creatures could arise
And multiply themselves to many times their size?
To whom should life be thankful, to Darwins or to gods,
That from the struggle upward, against all unlikely odds,
There came at last a creature, perhaps one meant to be,
That from these vicious ways turned into you and me?

Yes, cruel is what we were, and what we still remain,
Feeding on the life's lesser forms is built into the brain,
But now those lesser forms are vanishing too fast,
And if we are to carry on, alas it's come to past,
That we must feed upon—and take and do not give—
All creatures *just like us* so we alone can live.
How can we justify such selfish sin?
Is killing one another the only way to win?
The only answer I can give, the vicious way we are
Is also the arrangement that let us come this far.
So we can use our vicious brains to let us think and be
Beings who can also love—as I love you and you love me—
Beings who can think so well we'll somehow reach that day
When we will conquer viciousness, and live another way.

You Cannot Blow Away the Sodden Leaves

You cannot blow away the leaves
The rain has soaked to sodden sludge.
At least you hope the leaves that lie beneath the coming snow
That once, in all their beauty, hung upon the autumn trees,
And now must fight the winter freeze,
Will lie beneath the snow to wait to give a nudge
To life, through slow decay, and then they'll bring
New life again to light in early spring.

What is a Mountain?

What is a mountain, merely a scenic view?
Or a stairway to Heaven that we can walk upon too?
A climber's challenge, eons without breath,
A moment of glory, followed by death,
A god of the ancients, the Lord of the Earth,
From whom gods below were all given birth,
That descended to humans, who look now to the sky
And worship the Father who rules from on high?

All of these are a mountain, either an ice-covered stone
Or a stupa where a god is personified
As a mountain that reigns from his throne.
Whatever the truth, when raising our eyes,
If mountains aren't there to behold
Something vital within us dies.

Miami Heat

I'm back at home in Miami,
And the heat is more than just warm
But it's not just the heat that is hurting,
The humidity does most of the harm.

I should have stayed in the mountains
Yes, I know it's now very cold.
But the heat down here will kill me,
In the mountains, I will merely grow old.

Arden Forests Legends

The Forests of Arden have legions of legends
Of beauteous maidens and eager young knights,
Of evil old crones, who tempted the lovers,
And then made them regret their forbidden delights.

My new Bedford forests also have legends
Of Indian maidens and eager young braves,
But American forests don't whisper their fables—
All of the tellers are long in their graves.

I roam through these forests and savor the silence,
Hoping to hear a word from the past,
But all that I hear is wind through the arbors
And even that sadness is not fated to last.

When Our Words Sing
The Heart Takes Wing

It then occurs to one of the guests—thank goodness—that someone went to a lot of trouble to prepare this excellent meal, so to show appreciation, questions are asked about recipes, and the chef gets a chance to pontificate. How did he get started, from whom did he learn, what did he learn in the process of becoming a chef, and what clever tricks did he employ to make the various dishes even tastier?

All of which parallels the mastering of the art of writing poems, so here are some of the ways I prepared your poetic meal.

Aurora Borealis

I was lonely and empty, afraid of the future,
And no longer a believer in God,
Stationed to the north, protecting my country,
Though not on American sod.

I had longed to be heard, a user of words,
A novelist and a poet as well,
But all that I'd written was as legible as hen tracks,
And I didn't even know how to spell.

I was twenty years old, on a barren hilltop,
Awaiting the first winter snow.
Since the sky was too clear, I was startled instead—
Aurora borealis was beginning its show.

Bright shafts of color thrust up from the Northland,
Purple, yellow, crimson and green.
God, the Artist, with the sky as His canvas,
Was painting a heavenly scene.

Wordless in wonder, freezing yet burning,
I pondered what this painting could mean,
But, though seeming forever, yet all too soon,
It vanished as a vision not seen.

Something then ended on that Canadian hilltop,
I was no longer what I'd been before.
A new me was born who was open to wonder,
And eager for what next lay in store.

Continued . . .

I still was not certain that God was the artist,
    Or that God even existed at all,
But with or without Him, *someone's* wonder
    Had given me a wake up call.

I'd ascend from my hilltop, unafraid of the future,
    To become an artist of the word.
Using paper as canvas, by the light of the heavens,
    I'd tell all the world what I'd heard.

The Words Will Nourish Me

Certain things must be, to make a poem,
    The talent and the skill to use the word
To paint a picture never seen before
In sounds of feelings the world's never heard.

If this poet has courage and also the will
    To *live* feelings and use talent and skill,
    At least one poem may come to be
    That will entrance, amaze, and thrill,
A banquet of words to enrich the reader
    And also to nourish me.

Creating Reality with Words

Nothing even existed before
I created reality with words.
Then I created the heavens,
And filled my heaven with birds,
Then I created oceans,
Then the creatures beneath the sea,
Then I created the forests,
Then finally I created Me.

What do I think I am doing?
Do I think that I am the God
Who creates all reality?
No, I am only doing
What God no longer need do—
Making a different Me—
And words are the godlike tools
That I use in my *self*-creating
Creativity.

The Successful Poem

The successful poem is one to which the reader reacts,
"Oh yes, I knew that!"
Or it reaches into the reader's head
And finds what is wise, and brings it out—
Too often *my* readers say, instead,
"What in hell was that all about?"

Words Are Wilting Flowers

Poets have responsibility
To use word-versatility.
Words are wilting flowers
That time has abused.
Words too often used
Also lose their beauty,
And all of their poetic powers,
To make what has been abused
Into new, ever-blooming word-flowers.

So I hope *I* have shown word-facility
And done my poetic duty
Showing responsibility
In poetic versatility.

Rhymed and Unrhymed Poems

Rhymed and unrhymed poems are both okay,
But it's best not to compare them.
They both use words to express ones feelings,
If one have courage enough to bare them.

Rhyming poems are songs that sing to me,
And I love to share them.
Unrhymed poems are like gifts I appreciate,
But seldom enough to wear them.

I Want My Poems to Sing

I want my poems to sing.
Yes, they can have meaning without rhythm and rhyme,
But with such musical devices my poems will take wing,
And something even better than meaning
Will travel through time,
So it's this meaning beyond meaning
To the world I am trying to bring.

Two O'clock in the Morning

It's two o'clock in the morning,
And words come on without warning,
May these foolish thoughts I am spawning
Make better sense at dawning!

The Practice of Poetry

Learning to write poetry is like learning to play the violin,
The violinist must put his fingers to the bow everyday,
And the poet must put his fingers to the pen—
Again, and again, and again.
That's the only way
The violinist can play perfectly every time,
And the long-practicing poet can find
The almost perfect rhyme.

Reading a Poem

When reading a poem, the unexpected is expected,
What is obviously one thing is metaphorically something else.
Words are carefully selected
To clearly express a thought, that magically melts
Into ambiguity before the poem moves in a new direction,
That, in the end, will reveal to the reader
What the poet actually intended,
All of which justifies the poet's clever selection
Of words and phrases that are often open-ended—
But only if the reader is given by the poetic master-crafter,
A modicum of wisdom or at least a moment of laughter.

I'm Complaining About Your Complaining

Writers of verse, or non-verse, who call yourselves a poet,
I'm complaining about your complaining.
According to you, life's all bad,
And only you have the wisdom to know it.
I shouldn't think this would need explaining:
Considering the infinitesimal chance
That we're even here at all—

Continued ...

An unlikely event in space,
Or some god's somehow making the call—
The blessings of life ever since
On our heads have been a-raining.
So spew out your verse, using wiser words this time,
Without rhythm and even without rhyme,
And thank your lucky stars you're living at all
To call yourself a poet.

It's Time to Not Write a Poem

It's time to not write a poem,
It's time to not have the great thought,
It's time for the Muses to be absent,
It's time to not care what's not wrought.

Don't worry what thoughts your are missing
In this moment that you are not writing.
It's true what is *not* being written
Will not be like writing—exciting.

But it might be that what later you'll write
Will be something you'd overlook seeing
If you'd spent all your time at your poem
Instead of spending a few moments just being.

Oh my, I am so hypocritical,
As a hypocrite, I couldn't be worse.
While promising I'd not write a poem
I was putting silly thoughts into verse.

Gloves and Books

Gloves and books are much alike,
They are chosen for your protection.
Hands must not touch what would poison the body,
And be careful of your books selection.
For foreign thoughts might enter the mind
And cause a mental infection.
So sterilize what enters you eyes,
And submit to a censor's inspection,
Before it poisons your weakened thinking,
Lest your mind and body be sent below
Where patients in peril line up in a row
For old Doctor Devil's disinfection.

When Reading My Poems Aloud

When I read my poem aloud,
I want to see a reaction.
Frankly, my poetry readings
Are for *personal* satisfaction.

I want the listener to smile,
Or laugh, or sometimes to cry.
I want them to get so angry
They want me or someone else to die.

I want to force them to think,
Even about the reality of death,
Yet, somehow still to be happy
When drawing that one final breath.

Continued . . .

The one thing I don't want from listeners
Is indifferent nods of the head.
If this is all I can get from my listeners,
I'd sooner my poems went unread.

The Perfect Poem

A poem, to be a poem, must always be predictable.
It tells what you always knew, but in a novel way.
Great poems tell you what you thought you knew,
    But didn't really know—
Until the poem's perfection had its say.

And when the final line sums what you know is true.
A universal certainty has been revealed to you.
And this eternal truth, revealed to you that day,
Could only have been said exactly in that way.

So listen to this summary, predicting what I'll say.
Of course this poem's not perfect, but if I have my way
    You'll end it with the proper word,
    And thus you'll make my ____.

Words Are My Music

If I could make music like Schubert,
My voice would swell from my throat,
And I would sing like an angel,
And hearts would thrill to each note.

But I don't have Schubertic genius,
From me, musical notes are not heard.
Instead, I will play on your heartstrings
With the rhythm and sounds of a word.

I may not have talent for music,
But the poems I will sing out to you
Will be my own kind of music—
And when my singing is through,
I hope you'll be singing too.

Omar, You Intoxicate Me
After Edward FitzGerald

Wake! For the light of a brilliant mind
Rises out of the East to strike me blind,
Yet opens my eyes to the love of life
And bids me to drink all the joy I can find.

Omar Khayyam you intoxicate me,
Of course with your wine and your poetry,
But neither of these is the magic brew,
It's your joy in living that's setting me free.

"A book of verse underneath the bough"
While feeding on love, and never mind how,
In the wilderness, or wherever, who cares,
Once again, to your wisdom, I happily bow.

Yet, while you wallowed in a life without care,
Living on wine and the desert air,
Your thirsty mind sought to understand
The beginnings of life and the journey from there.

But the answers you found did not satisfy,
And the wisdom of ages seemed no more than a lie,
And the sages who taught became bones in the sand
Who none will remember when all of us die.

Continued . . .

So we work till the pain digs deep in the bone,
And little is left of our work that's our own.
Take what cash there is offered and let credit go—
Trees don't bare fruit that flower alone.

Never mind trees and the fruit they won't bear,
Never mind teachings, the wisdom's not there.
Repair to the tavern, where your friends drink their fill.
Those suffering with you are the ones who will care.

For the finger of fate writes your future in stone,
Though you beg for mercy and whimper or moan,
You cannot change what the die has cast,
For sins you committed you can never atone.

So you took up your goblet and drank with a will,
But left a few drops for those under the hill,
For ashes of drinkers were mixed with the sand,
Though bodies were gone they were thirsting there still.

But, Omar, I'll do better. Yes, before I too pass,
I'll find the place where you lie under grass,
And popping the cork, I'll drink to your spirit,
Then turn down my still brimming glass.

Is This Music?

Is what I hear music, or is it just noise?
Do I hear singers, or just blaring boys?
This much I know, when it enters my ears,
I never feel rapture, instead, I shed tears.

Whatever happened to the British Boy's Choir?
They were angelic, they could inspire,
And open my mind, and gladden my heart.
The loud group makes agony, the choir made art.

Nevermore

The raven was mocking me high up in the trees.
What was I doing down there on my knees
Stabbing the earth with a dark iron pick?
He cursed me and claimed that my brain must be sick.
But I planned to uproot and bring his tree down
To make that brash raven tumble down on his crown,
And then I would clutch him and bark in his face
And make him confess for the rest of his race,
"You weren't just a bust above an old door
So what did you mean when you croaked, "Nevermore!"?

But the bird that I longed for remained in the sky.
For his tree was too broad and its top was too high.
Though I dug there all day, I eventually found
Not the bird, but my vanity had come tumbling down.
So I trudged away sadly, my pick at my side,
But more than my vanity that day had just died.
All poets, now and future, were doomed to not know
What "Nevermore" might mean
To poor weak and all-weary Edgar A. Poe.

. . .

Let the punishment fit the crime,
If the lines don't end in rhyme,
Fell the phony to his knee
And hang him on the Poet-Tree.

This is Not a Poem
That Shakespeare Would Have Written

Suppose our famed Immortal Bard
Had found himself on stage again,
Within a glowing Globe, with strobbing lights,
Where sounds were painfully intensified,
And greenish vapors filled the air,
Where groundlings gathered there
To hear their gravel, grunting, rapping guru groan
About his wasted life, that drugs and booze
Had tumbled from its flawed and foolish heights
And now was in despair.

Suppose the Poet Personified,
Now standing still before those rows of mini minds,
Had softly then intoned,
"Shall I compare thee to a summer's day . . .?"
Would suddenly they hush, and wonder what had happened
To their whining, groaning rapper man
To whom they'd paid outrageous sums so they could hear
And cheer and be a fan?
Had he ascended high again and now was just as low?
And would they sigh and strain to see
Who questioned them,
This smallish, simply costumed-man
Who further asked, "To be or not to be . . ."?

And would they just as quietly ask,
"Be what? Be what? Please, answer if you can!"
And would a brief but puzzled look then form upon
This ghost from ages passed,
Who'd shake his head and quietly then have asked,
"Why be yourself, of course. What groundlings these
Who do not understand that birds upon the breeze

Have answers that confound the sad and silly man
Who stands before you now, who also wonders how
He has returned to take another bow?"

And then, of course, the mob, at last aroused,
Would raucously disdain this strange performing man,
And Shakespeare, nodding sadly there, would gladly seek
His Sixteenth Century grave
And leave behind these modern mindless groundlings
So he wouldn't have to hear them rave,
Until their modern star arose again
To give old Bill one final shove,
Stomping on his Yoric-loving skull, ". . .from time to time...
But not for love."[*]

[*]*"Men have died from time to time, and worms have eaten them, but not for love."*
William Shakespeare

In Praise of Lilting Lovely Lyrics
(After Gerard Manley Hopkins)

Lilting lovely lyrics are lights that leaven Heaven
And we are down below where life will have no leaven.
So in the dappled days delights
Then spawned beneath the dawning sun,
The songs you sing will soothe our souls
And of our grief un-grieve us.
I thank you lilting lyrics,
Your loving lays did not deceive us.

Continued . . .

Writing

When a book is done, I'm number one,
But what to do now? I don't know how
To begin again so I'll have the same fun
When my next book of poems is done.

But waiting to start is not very smart,
So just kick into gear and overcome fear,
And take on the bout to see what comes out,
For that is what writing should be all about.

Ode to Joy
(Compliments to Schiller and Beethoven)

Hear my voice rise up like thunder,
Shouting to the stars above.
I could feel no greater wonder
Than to hear you speak of love.
Hear my heart now bursting asunder,
Pouring forth the love I feel.
When I wake upon the morrow,
I'll just pray this night was real.

How could someone draped in beauty
Give her heart to one like me?
Why would someone made of starlight
Shed her light for me to see?
How could someone shining in Heaven
Be someone who's also real
Life's at last my Earthly Heaven,
Feeling how I've come to feel.

May I hope we'll join now together,
Sharing joy throughout each day,
Joined in life to love on forever.
When our bodies fade away,
Back among your stars we will settle,
For all life on Earth to see,
Love's symbolic constellation
Shinning through eternity.

No Coolin' Breeze
After Folk Music

There's a cool breeze a-comin'
And there are no banjos stummin'
And there ain't no old folks hummin'
As they wait that awful day.

And here's the dreadful reason,
It's now deseasin' season.
The Devil's now a-seizen
Old soul's to drag away.

And all that's left that's pleasing
Is down there, ain't no freezing.'
There'll be no coolin' breezing
When the Devil rules the day.

Devil Take You, Irishman

Finegen, Finegen, you're living in sin again
And the Devil is waiting downtown.
So go out tonight and have more delight,
Then the Devil will know where you've been again
And gleefully drag you on down.

Tautology and Oxymoron

Tautology and Oxymoron
When out to play one day,
And this is what this prankish pair
Invented on their way:
An empty vacuum, burning cold,
Fell into a solid hole.
Where living death made fearing bold
And all was new and very old.
But truthful lies can now be told,
An open space did then unfold
And broke apart, remaining whole.
So shut your eyes and you will see
A model of "tautology,"
And what is just the opposite,
Two words that do, but do not fit,
'Cause they are contradictory.
And also complimentary.
And you can see 'cause you are blind,
Unless you seek somewhere defined
Some wily words sunk in your mind,
The oxymorons you won't see
Nor the only one tautology.

Für Elise
In the rhythm of this little poem/ there will be/
A melody.
He who wrote each scared note/ was who wrote
A symphony.
What you will hear, your ears will please.
The song is called/ the Für Elise/
The Für Elise.

184

When this bird begins his little song,/   you might hear/
It all night long.
He is called the mockingbird/   Who's he mock/
ing in his song?
The master of/   all symphonies,
Who also wrote/   the Für Elise,/
The Für Elise.

When the mockingbird's in *silent* flight,/   it's a most/
Depressing thing.
But at times he will alight./   Then you'll hear/
The angels sing,
And from your head/   down to your knees
You soon will *feel*/   the Für Elise,/
The Für Elise.

When this warbling bird begins to sing/   you will feel
The warmth of spring.
As he sings his sacred song,/   an Ode to Joy/
Is what he'll bring.
And when the sun/   surmounts the trees,/
You still will hear/   the Für Elise,/
The Für Elise.

The End of the World is a-Coming
A Rhythmic Sermon

The end of the world is a-coming,
And damnation's a-stalking again.
The end of the world is a-coming,
And we've been a-living in sin.

Continued . . .

The Master ha' promised salvation,
If we'll do as we has been told.
The Master ha' promised salvation,
But our sin has a-taken a-hold.

We must attend to his teachings
And know all the things he has taught.
We must adhere to his preaching
Or we is a-cometh to naught.

The end of the world is a-coming,
In sin we must no longer roam.
If we'll just a-worship his coming,
The Master will welcome us home.

Useless Words?
I grasp a word that fails, but still I try.
I cast the word aside, but it won't die.
It lies within my hidden mind, and while I sleep,
It blends with other words to wildly leap
Into a thought so wonderful and wise
The words become a poem that never dies.

And so each day I store each useless word
And let it live, though it may be absurd.
The wisdom that I've learned, *Don't criticize*
Until you learn where wisdom truly lies.

Never Mind That Significant Sonnet

Using poetry to simplify
But hint at the great troubling truth
Might have made me a model poet,
But now I'm too long in the tooth.

But all of a sudden, I realize
That the thought above is quite wise,
So now that I've come upon it,
I'll don my thinking bonnet
To write a sonnet on it.

But as I start, with so much at stake,
The thinking only makes my old tooth ache—
Oh well, never mind that significant sonnet,
I'll just keep it under my bonnet.

The Spenserian Stanza

I'll write a verse the Edmund Spenser way.
Ten beats per line, one short and then one long.
Perhaps an ode, or better yet a song
To lighten hearts and lift them through the day.
And with this verse I'll drive your pain away.
I'll make all right, all things you felt were wrong.

Though you were weak, you'll now be hale and strong.
So now I've had my Edmund Spenser say.
With Spenser's extra beat, this line has not now
gone astray.

Great Operas Have Gone Away

Peony! Peony!
Wails the tenor,
Madama Butterfly has flown away.

Peony! Peony!
Why's he wailing?
He has no choice—it's in the play.

Continued . . .

Peony! Peony!
Has finished dying,
Pinkerton no longer wails.

Peony! Peony!
A diva's dying's
A common thing in opera tales.

Peony! Peony!
But *I'm* still crying.
Why don't my tears now fade away?

Puccini, Puccini
Has ceased composing,
And that's the end of "One Fine Day."

Suppose There had Never Been Art

Suppose there're had never been music,
Or stories, or novel, or plays,
And words, and pencils, and paint
Were used only in literal ways

To depict the world as it is.
Or what science could prove what could be,
And still we had made great progress
In creating all the things that you see.

Then one day I composed the first poem,
About something that had never been,
About feelings both mournful and joyous
And whatever might come to be then.

When others then heard of this wonder,
This immaterial and unreal fantasy,
Would they honor this thing called a poem
Or would they frantically get rid of me?

I suspect, whatever my fate,
Be it fame or quick crucifixion,
My offering them what might have been
Would result in this certain prediction:

The material man would grow,
But feelings would undergo change,
And the familiar material world
Would turn into something more strange.

The feelings would no longer be moderate,
They would range from the high to the low,
And the future could never be known,
For we'd go, then, wherever we'd go.

So that's the choice we would make,
Do only what can be controlled,
Or let loose free-art on the world
And let what's frightfully unknown just unfold.

The Boom Box is Booming

The boom box is booming!
My head hurts like hell,
I'll bong the musician.
He'll gong like a bell.

I've done it, he's quieter,
I've regained my day,
His musical madness
Is fading away . . .

Words Make Real

When listening to these words,
 Do childhood scenes awake?
You're running through a field,
  Or wading in a stream,
  Or rolling down a hill,
  Or swimming in a lake,
  Or flying through the air,
 Then waking in a dream,
 Knowing that you sleep,
 Yet knowing that it's real

  If only you'll lie still,
 The dawn would stay away
And you can dream until,
 The happiness you feel
 Rises from these words,
 To make a perfect day.

Aging is When
You Remember to Begin Again

The meal and our evening together are almost over. We'll have our desert just before parting. That thought, of course, brings on a little sadness. The happier our time together, the sadder we might be to depart.

Not that we didn't have our minor disagreements during the evening. In our brief time as fellow diners, there might have even been moments when we wished that we hadn't come at all. The same is true for lifetime relationships, sometime we wonder if they should have ever begun. But just as we mellowed with good food and wine, we also mellow with aging, and being mellower and wiser, we might be able to discover other ways of looking at leaving, even the final leaving. Let's explore together.

Purpose in Aging

This growing old is something new for me,
I haven't been here before.
It wasn't what I experienced,
As I emerged through living's first door.
Now, there're times on the way,
When I wonder what's come into play,
And what I am becoming,
And even if I should I continue to stay.

Of course, I will stay alive,
So I must encounter this strange new me.
I'll accept these new limits and pain
That are part of what I'd come to be.
As a youth, my death was a probable,
Now my death is a certainty,
And I have to live each day of my life
With death as my company.

In my youth, I had one paramount goal—
Find a mate to bear progeny.
Now my lineage is provided for,
What goal is still left for me?
Yes, I'll accept each day as it comes,
With its limits and moments of pain
And use what wisdom I've garnered
To accept what else may remain.

Continued . . .

But I hope that this new older me
Will still have a reason to live,
And, as my limitations increase,
I'll still have a few things to give,
And when even that goal is over,
I'll look forward, as others before,
To learn if living had purpose,
As I go through life's last final door.

Growing Old is Not So Hot

This growing old is not so hot.
I'm now without power, so I relax a lot,
But none of the young-ones will listen to me.
They think that they know
All it took me so many years to see.
I'd like to return to my elevated spot
On top of the heap so I could stir the pot
To show those smart young ones they're not so smart.
I'd show them that leading's a long-practiced art,
And they'd better start listening before I am gone,
Or they'll just be repeating all the things I did wrong.

Sleep

Sleep, Oh Sleep, you do not come easy.
I'll do most anything, praise thee, please thee,
If you'll just enfold me in your blanket of love.
Do not torment me, I have enough of
Those agonies in daylight, I need none at night.
Instead, please delight me with your soft gentle shove
Out of the wrongness that keeps me awake
And into the darkness whose touch will make rightness
That turns into light that shows me the way
To emerge recovered to face the new day.

Dreams of My Childhood

I remember the dreams of my childhood,
They hinted at happiness ahead.
Though they faded each morning,
The hope that they heralded
Always remained in my head.
Those dreams of the past have now vanished,
Friends soon departed, and hopes went astray,
So when I awake in the morning,
And heartaches have now been heralded,
I'm glad that those dreams fade away.

Avoiding an Adult Accident

Woe is me! Woe is me! In the night, I woke painfully,
And urgently needing to pee.
So I dragged my old frame to the toilette
So with my pee I could painfully soil it.
If I'd wet my bed before I got to the head,
My smarty-pants grandkids
Would make mean weewee fun of me.

Remembering Names

Purslane and John Wayne are names
That are firmly fixed in my brain,
But I cannot remember the same
Of that poet who lived overzealously
But later died sorrowfully in shame.

Continued . . .

Think of "The Ballad of Reading Goal"
And "The Picture of Dorian Gray."
His name's almost there in my porous head
And then instantly flitters away,
And I am concerned, that hampered with age,
My memory won't be able or willing to stay.

And when I try to remember, I'm almost in rage,
But the faint foolish thoughts are still never there.
They have vanished like ephemeral bubbles
That go "Pop!" in the warm summer air.

So give me a hand, and try if your will
To remember that name, if your brain holds it still,
Or will old age defeat you, and you'll also be
Mad empty minded, feeling foolish like me?

My Life is One Long List of Used-to-Be's

I used to be a therapist, a sort of non-frocked preacher.
I used to be a lover, but not while being teacher.
I used to be an athlete, always flying through the air.
I used to be a looker, but now I have no hair.

I used to be a writer, with several books to show it.
I used to be, and hope this poem won't blow it—
Please tell me that you know it— I still can be a poet.

A Chill That Fills Me

There's a chill that fills me
That's not from winter or the dark of the sun.
It's an ache in my heart and a night in my mind,
That raises these questions my doubt has begun:

Why was I trying, why did I care?
Why did I wonder if I should be there?
Why was I lonely, with love by my side?
What will come after when thinking has died?
When I'm just ashes they've spread o're the sea,
Who was that nothing who never was me?

This is the chill, the unending cold,
The absence of meaning that rules, now I am old,
At least I am certain, in this emptiness that's me,
Others have journeyed this lone way before,
Come in and gone out of this very same door,
And wherever they went, that's where I will be.
I just pray that those others are now waiting for me.

Granny Broxton's Message

Granny Broxton died without my standing by her side.
And then the message came to me that, on the night she died,
She'd asked, specifically, that I be there with her,
That she had words to speak, and would prefer
That I alone would hear those words. Till then, she'd stall.
But I had other things to do, and did not heed her call.

She could not wait, the one who called for her
Would never hesitate, and didn't care what she'd prefer.
Now years have come and gone, and I have words as well.
And children of my children, to you these words I'll tell.
I wonder if the wisdom that Granny held for me
Were just the words, my children, I'll pass along to thee.
I'll never know, I was not there, but that's *my* tragedy,
And maybe yours as well—
Unless you chose to spend my final hour with me.

Winter Rain

Ancient body, racked in pain!
Why complain, what's the gain?
Youth is like a summer rain,
Once it's fallen down the drain,
It won't see the sun again.
Age, for all it's painful strain,
Feels more like a winter rain.
Once it's started, like the pain,
There's no end, so why complain?

The Human Brain's an Amazing Thing

The human brain's an amazing thing!
Even when it's insane, it can hear a ring,
It can see a star, it can feel your feet,
It can tell your mouth what you shouldn't eat

It can tell your body that you're gaining weight,
It can make you worry when you wake too late,
It knows the difference between loving and just lust,
Love lies in the bosom and does not leer at a bust,
It can tell your gonads that now it's time to act,
Then keep your lust from straying from the proper track.

My human brain, although it's still quite sane,
And its long life of thinking is almost through,
Has just one awkward thing that it can never do,
That's remember people's names now it's seventy-two.

Happiness Can Harm

When I become too happy,
I sometimes lose my mind,
And if I am not careful
Reason's left behind.

I know I should be smarter,
Happiness can harm.
For when the joy's departed,
What's sad begins to swarm.

That's when I'll need the mind
That I had thrown away,
To prove that being happy
Will come another day.

But now I am not listening,
I'm *choosing* to be blind
I cannot be this happy
Unless I lose my mind.

Open Another Door

Thank God, it's time for closure,
I can't handle a moment more.
But if I am to go on growing,
Every moment of closure
Must open another door.

It's Time to Go

It's time to go.
I have no reason now to reach the end of just another day.
How do I know?
I feel no hope that other reasons will appear along the way.
I hear no call
Assuring me that I alone can do whatever must be done,
And that is all
I need to know, so I will wait to greet my final setting sun.
It's time to go.

Another Place

When the moon is in full on a cloudless night,
Then no cloudlets can shadow its opal light,
So whatever darkens its shining face
Must come from the Earth—or another place,

I stand below on a barren plain,
I was here before and I've come again,
And I am too small to shadow the moon,
And the one once with me has left me too soon.

Yet, across the face of that great haunted orb
Flowed a shadow too quick for my mind to absorb
And that shade took the form of the one who had flown,
Then fled in a moment, and left me alone.

I have only one choice, my pain is too great,
Life without love is too terrible a fate.
To see once again that long missing face,
I'll abandon the Earth—for that other place.

Leaves Are Like Hair

Leaves falling in autumn,
Are foretelling the falling of snow,
And that fair days are passing,
And earth will be frozen below.

And the falling of hair's like falling of leaves
That's letting me know
That my fair days are passing and, like earth,
I soon will be frozen below.

Assisted Living

I have toured an old folks home,
By its modern euphemistic, sometimes called Assisted Living.
What a horrible experience I had there.
Here's the lesson it was giving:
I saw creatures feces-sitting, mewling, moaning, drooling,
And no one who watched them writhing seemed to care,
As these bodies, time had broken,
With their frames so frail and fragile,
Dangled sideways from a more decrepit chair.

You, who claim to have the power,
When my ending is approaching,
Send me straight on down to Hades.
Yes, no doubt it will be painful, and an agony unending,
But compared to what I witnessed,
I'll be happy, happy, there.

With Death Abide

With Death abide.
Mount upon his stallion.
What fate had promised long ago
Cannot be denied,
No matter how unwisely and courageously you tried.

Now urge your steed to cantor, and break into a gallop
Then race across the darkened plain.
The past is passed, the future never was,
And *now*, as ever more, has come again.
But see you not a distant spot of light
Beyond the edge of night
That brightens into blinding dawn?

Then on its own, the stallion slows its frantic pace
And softly sets its hooves upon
A carpet emerald lawn,
And slowly kneels that you may slide from off its back
To stand upon your feet,
As it boldly retreats to leave this place,
For this steed of Death had now run its race.

Then that which came before your life and death
Has come again,
So in that mystery that's yet to be revealed,
Awhile abide.
Perhaps this time you will not be beguiled
To think that Death should *ever* be reviled.

Someday Like Them

I hardly paid much attention to these old folks before,
The fragile, the decrepit, the dim.
Lately, I'm beginning to stare, and more carefully compare
And worry that I'll *someday* be like them.
And then it comes to me, considering history,
Someday, even the longest journey ends.
Then it traumatizes me, when I look again and see,
Some of those ancient folks
Were my closest childhood friends.

Alzheimer

I always hoped for more than this,
With loved ones waiting at my side.
To each I'd give a parting kiss.
They'd know my love had never died.

But who are these beside my bed?
I can't recall, I know not how.
And who am I, whose past is dead,
Who fades into eternal now?

And who are you to cruelly chose
To take away my dignity?
If I choose death, what will *you* lose?
What right have you to chose for me?

If I live on without a mind,
Without a past, no history,
I only know that you will find
That emptiness will not be me.

Continued . . .

While I still have my working mind,
It is my choice, let me decide.
Just stand aside, God is not blind,
He knows that I've already died.

It Wasn't Your Death

It wasn't your death that disturbed me,
But the painful way of it,
To choke on food that should nourish you
And then grasp for breath
To curse the life that you threw away
Because you could not love it,
And then in your final moments, that horrifying surprise
That told the world you had told yourself
Those self-destroying lies.
Well Son, I'll say goodbye to you,
And my heart will nonetheless break,
But I feel this, not for you,
But for your abandoned children's sake,
And I pray that they and I, though marked by death,
Will rise above it.

Hollow House

Not even a mouse, with a caring spouse,
Would want to live
In hollow house.
Not even a wife could lighten his life
In hollow house.
There'd be no yummies to tighten their tummies
In hollow house.
The rooms would be dark, and lonely and stark
In hollow house.

And not even lice would live on these mice
In hollow house.
And so it's not clear, why I am still here.
Why I still live
In hollow house.
I once had a wife who abandoned this life
In hollow house.
I'm frozen inside, and wished I had died
In hollow house.
So why don't I leave, instead of just grieve
In hollow house?
I fear it's too late, I guess I'll just wait,
And live with my fate
In hollow house.

Kenny

While he lived, what he did was most grievous,
And we hated how this made him behave,
For he drank, and then tried to deceive us.
But, alas, now he's gone to his grave,
We remember instead how he loved us
Before his drinking took hold,
How he placed no others above us,
And his caring that never grew old.
What The Bard once said, though quite clever,
Was untrue, and *this* truth I hope you now save,
The good that men do lives forever,
It's the evil that's interred in the grave.

An Elegy for an Ordinary Man

Death has come among us, and not the metaphoric death
The elegiac poets so often praised when, in the public gaze,
Their icon drew his final breath, to end his fame-filled days.
    I hereby mark the death of just an ordinary man,
One who some of us had loved and who had often irritated
    Those he loved but who, when death was in the plan,
    Was then revered so that we spoke but loving words
When standing by his grave and promised we would not forget
The man whom he had been, or could have been—and yet,
    Like all the promises we make when mired in grief,
    This was a way we only hoped we could behave—
    But needs of daily living lay our loved one
    Even deeper in his grave.

But let me praise this ordinary man, as he is laid to rest,
    And speak with greater honesty
    Than used in elegies the olden poets gave
For those revered and sacred icons of departed days.
    "Now here me, too soon forgotten one,
    I know you tried to do your best,
And when you failed, you tried and tried again,
And that is good enough to earn my praise.

I honor you, departed one,
And know that when we meet again,
In brighter days, with all of those who had been in your plan,
    To gather 'neath the sun before we go our separate ways,
    That you will praise me there as also *just an ordinary man.*"

Why Not?

Much work was done today.
I guess that you can say, "That's good!"
But then there always comes the question,
"Why?"
Why should I even do the work that I have done today?"
And then the only answer that I've got
To this perennial question, "
Is my perennial answer, "Why? Why not?"

So till I die,
I'll always answer this infernal "Why?"
With the only answer that I've got,
My eternal, all encompassing answer—
"Oh well, what the hell, why not!"

Where are the Myths of the Past?

Where are the elves who enchanted me?
Where are the spirits who haunted my dreams?
Where are the mermaids who swam in the sea?
Where are the goblins with their hideous screams?

Gone to the West with all myths of the past
That gave my life meaning, though they mist-filled my mind,
Science replaced them, and science will last—
But, alas, they left voids where Science is blind.

I Should Have Died When I Was Young

Yes, something is amiss, I should have died
When I was young, before I reached my prime,
A work in progress by my death denied,
A tragedy interred in earth before his time.

The world could say, "What poetry might have come
If Death had only spared this budding mind."
Instead, the Heartless Dread had struck me dumb,
And promises are all that I had left behind.

Oh well, I have not wasted all my time.
I've used my many years to work and write.
And I have loved and set my love to rhyme.
Those loves will weep when I pass into night.

So do not say I lived too long—be glad—
Since what I did, with time, was not so bad.

Together or Alone

We always knew it had to come to this,
The good, the bad, there had to be an end.
Forget the sad, remember happiness,
And let the anger vanish like the wind.

The road ahead may have no certain signs,
And falling darkness makes it hard to see,
And we must struggle up some steep inclines
Before we reach where we are meant to be.

It would be good to have some certainty,
But destiny is not designed that way.
The future isn't fixed, we cannot see
What waits beyond that fateful final day.
We now must choose, the seeds of time are sown.
We either go together or alone.

Always With You

As each of my body functions fade away
Will I still continue as me?
Was I never more than the sum of my parts
And is that all I will ever be?

Or do all these parts, merely physical,
Sum to something that somehow stays
When all my parts have returned to earth
And gone their separate ways?

I hope that when you come seeking,
Call it soul or call it mind,
You'll find more than just the physical,
A thing eternal that's been left behind.

And then you'll hear the words I've spoken
And know that what I said was true,
The promises I made were not broken—
Eternal me will be ever with you.

Beyond the Midnight Light

The light of midnight lit the sky.
I knew my time had come to die.
I wanted reasons, it told me how,
It told me where, but never why.

The light was beauty, the light was sad,
The light was painless, so I was glad.
It spread before me all I had done,
And I was ending where I'd begun.

It showed me others who mourned my fate,
Who meant to love me but came too late.
I tried to tell them, my voice a sigh,
That at the end I *had* learned why.

In passing over, beyond the light,
A day was dawning that had no night.
Of loneliness, I now was free,
For *you've* at last returned to me.

The Sound of Hope

I shall not hear these sounds again:
The serenade of tree frogs through the night,
The lapping waves on sand when tide comes in
The buzz of bees through flowers bright.
The whispered winds that stir the trees,
The babbling brook along the trail,
The autumn leaves that flutter in the breeze,
The moan of pain from limbs that fail.

And when the sounds no longer reach my ears,
And other sounds have faded from my mind,
Will pain alone condemn my final years,
Regretful groans be all that's left behind?
If this be true, then what were joyful sounds
Had set me up to feel this painful fall,
And life itself is something to despise,
As birth began the wearing of the pall.

But as I lie and contemplate my fate,
The precious sounds are still within my mind.
The pain, which haunts my nights of late,
Recedes, and hope is left behind.

So when the final silence sighs,
They'll come a sound that soothes away the grief—
The sounds were joys, they were not lies—
The sound I hear is my profound relief.

The Reaper Grim Left His Calling Card

The Reaper Grim left his calling card
The night I almost died.
"Sorry I missed you, I'll catch you again.
Others more urgently needed my ride."
So I never really met him back then,
But I can't really say that I'm sad
That I had been a most shameful host
Whose etiquette was just terribly bad.
And I'll then pray, that I'll be away
The next time that he calls.
But if he'd like, he may wait all night
Within my empty halls.

Continued . . .

For as long as I'm able I'll rise from my table
And run a mile or two.
Then at ninety-nine, we'll sit down and dine,
After which, Reaper, I'll then ride away with you.

The Tide Flows Out Again

Come in, Come in! I've been expecting you.
You missed the tide and spent the night at sea?
But now, at dawn, you are at last with me,
And I await what you have come to do.

The night has passed, the darkness fades away.
I'll feel your gentle kiss upon my cheek.
You bear the gift I never though I'd seek.
You'll say the words that only you can say.

Come in, come in, my door is opened wide.
I've donned the clothes the traveler must wear.
The past is done, I have no need to stay.
My eyes are closed, but with you at my side
I'll need no sight to know when I am there.
The tide flows out again, let's not delay.

In the Final Draft
The Wise Ones Laughed

Finally, the desert is served, and the chocolate delight is both sweet and somewhat bitter—as are the feelings that seep in when we accept that the soirée is over and, for some, this might be our last night together. But, it was a wonderful evening, and if we have developed a wise attitude over the years, we know that it has also been a wonderful life. So, let us celebrate rather than grieve as the final moments approach.

I Was Bound By Principles

I was bound by principles, in my earliest day,
That led me toward Heaven in the narrowest ways.
And just at the end when, alas, it's too late
Are there tidbits of sin on my near empty plate.
But I've gobble them down and loved them as well,
And for those few sins, I am burning in Hell.
How I wished I'd abandoned those principles in youth.
At least I'd have memories of a far funner truth.

In Praise of the Moment

This happy moment wasn't here before.
I opened a door and in I went,
And what I had been before that door
Doesn't matter. That time was spent
In getting me here, and where I go now
I do not care.
Now is here—I am not there.

Step in the Stream

Risk dipping your feet in the stream,
Without a risk, there's no need to dream,
Anyway, I'll make you're a reasonable bet,
That all that glitters will not always be wet,
And some risks may be less than they seem.

Leaving No Longer Grieves Me

It's one thing to have a way to live,
It's another to have a reason.
I've struggle to use what time will give,
But death will have its season.

I only hope I'll forestall the time
When reasons for living leave me.
When my body finally finishes the climb
And leavings no longer grieve me.

Death, You Came Too Late.

Why? I wonder why we do this.
My only answer, "'Screw this,
If all we do is wait to die
Until we slowly make it through this.

Perhaps there is another way,
Where life can have its say,
And you will live, and so will I
To celebrate another day.

So let's not sit around and wait.
We should not bow to fate.
In fact, we should not choose to die.
We'll just tell Death, "You came too late."

I'm Riding a Perilous Ridge

I am riding a perilous ridge, a precipice on either side.
One false step and I'll fall from that height
And plummet to a pit of eternal night
To dwell in Hell, though I've not yet died.

That's why I'm cautious, and take no chance
I make few mistakes, and those are all small.
But unfortunately, that's not how to grow tall,
And on top of my ridge, I will never dance.

But I'm weary of waiting, there's a new way I'll go.
I'll pick up speed, and run to the end
Though the path even narrows, and begins to ascend,
For a time, I will fly, as I fall down below.

What Will Become?

What will become of this aging man?
Nothing is now as it seemed before.
There is no way of knowing the way ahead,
Where birthing is supposed to have lead,
There was no dependable plan.
Must the way, once entered, exit the one final door,
Or continue a journey, with moments of magic to lighten the
way,
With souls touching souls, being more everyday,
And at last being one—
And beyond that, becoming far more?
Yes, what will become on that grand final day,
Something more unknowable than ever before?

Dying Young or Old

I hadn't planned to live so painfully long,
Dying young would have been easier than aging.
At death, I would still have been strong
And met parting without fear, and while raging.

But, alas, this all-lingering journey
Is filled with much weakness and pain,
And I lie like one glued to a gurney
With no reason to rise up again.

So what is the point in this long-living
In a body too frail to fight on
That has nothing left that's worth giving
And no reason to live past the dawn?

I give only these few words of wisdom
For the ones who are yet fearless and strong,
Be sure that your young life has no schism
Between young-death and living too long.

Live wisely while your young-life is flying
So long-life, when it comes as surprise,
Will be youthfully strong at its dying,
And you'll rage with regret when it dies.

Windblown Wisdom

Windblown wisdom, whistling by my brain
Says, wiser thought might never come again.
It's best I open up my mind
And let the past just fall behind
So future thoughts will not have been in vain.

What says this wind that now I hear?
"Don't listen to what others fear
If you just trust what's in your sight,
That black is black and white is white,
The truth of life will soon be clear.

"And though the end is still in sight,
And dawn will someday lead to night,
The wind that then is whistling by
Will tell you on the day you die,
"Have pride, old man, you did alright!"

My Twenty-Four Milestones

First I was born—my Milestone One—
I wasn't much there, but life had begun.

Then Milestone Two, first day at school,
Playtime is over, nuns will now rule.

Next, love's first kiss, at Milestone Three,
On dark back stairs, my cousin kissed me.

Continued . . .

Then Milestone Four, first graduation,
Fear of the future followed elation.

Next, Milestone Five, I alone cried,
Or it seemed that way when my Father died.

Wow! Milestone Six, I ran my best race.
I honored myself, though I won second place.

Moving down south, at Milestone Seven.
When being piss-poor, Florida's not Heaven.

Commencement began at Milestone Eight,
High school was over. Would college await?

No, first the Air Force, that's Milestone Nine,
Nights without women, then rise up and shine.

Mustering out, at Milestone Ten,
Four years of boredom, now live again!

Milestone Eleven, at last, FSU.
Those sweet Southern Bells! Those stories were true!

Milestone One-Two, again capped and gowned.
Not second place now, how's "Doctor" sound?

Milestone Thirteen, I'd take The Great Chance,
I'd love but one woman and give up romance.

Milestone fourteen, I'd done the right thing.
Our first child was born. What more could life bring?

Milestone Fifteen, my first "Doctor" work,
The pay is so measly, I think I'm a jerk.

Milestone Sixteen, I do psychotherapy—
Teaching my patients what I'd learned about me.

Milestone Seventeen, our children were grown.
Another great chance, let them go on their own?

Milestone Eighteen, great pain down my arm!
Though Death had come calling, I'd heard his alarm.

Milestone Nineteen. Now's time to retire.
What would I do when I couldn't climb higher?

Milestone Twenty, I finally could write,
As I'm doing right now, awake late at night.

Milestone Two and One, soon the journey is done.
Will I go someplace else, or where I'd begun?

The Unanswered Question, Milestone Two-Two,
Where am I going when this life is through?

Seeking the answer, Milestone Two-Three,
Are loves who've departed now waiting for me?

Knowing the answer, Milestone Two-Four,
The lid that's closing is an opening door!

Longevity's Not Too Brevity

Longevity 's not so wonderful
If now your life's all blunder full,
And life is full of medicine,
And you are bound in bed again.
Perhaps it's time you fled?

Continued . . .

But choosing-time has come around,
And you're not sure you're Heaven bound,
And Satan's lurking underground—
Perhaps you'll stay in Bed?

God's Grace

Warm sun on my head,
Cool breeze on my face,
If not God's Heaven,
At least it's His grace.
Soft grass beneath me,
In this holy place,
All cares and concerns
Leave not a trace.

All's Well, That Ends Well.
And We Heard Laughter When the Curtain Fell.

Goodbye, dinner guests and readers. I hope you've enjoyed yourself as much as I have. So here are a few parting thoughts—for your doggie bag, perhaps?

What Makes Work Important?

What's important, the happiness I feel when a task is done?
Or the excitement I feel when a new work's begun?
Or the joy in those thoughts never thought of before
That occur out of nowhere as I move through the chore?
Or perhaps this new work creates a new me,
And I can rejoice in what I've now come to be.
Or is it the thought, though I've never sought fame,
That those I respect will now honor my name?

No, now that I've thought the whole process through,
There's one thing that's certain, there's one thing that's true,
As long as I'm working, as long as I strive,
The importance of working is it keeps me alive.

Working Makes Me Happy

Working makes me happy.
Of course, it's the way I was raised.
You don't survive, you don't get ahead,
By lying all day in your bed.
So here I am in my seventies,
My regular work is now done,
But I still get up every morning—
My new kind of work has begun.

And when this new work is over,
I'll go where all good workers go.
I'll be welcomed in the Great Worker's Heaven,
And here's something I think you should know,
The Heavenly Boss will reward me,
For all of my work since my birth,
With the job of cleaning up Heaven
So that all the new souls can be spotless
When we send them to awake down to the Earth.

Index

Contents

About the Author

D. B. Clark is a retired Clinical Psychologist, and Professor, and the author of *The Way to L'vei, The End of Ohm, A Heaven of Hell, Self-Development and Transcendence, Ashes to Ashes, Thoughts Along the Way, The Way Beyond, Mother Rat & Love is Eternal, Left of the Right World, On the Shoulders of Giants, Clever Quotes from Ancient Throats, It could be Verse, Poor Richard Returns, Forever Young, Death, a Second Opinion,* and *Love and Roses.* Check the author's web site, dbclark.com for further information, and iuniverse.com and lulu.com for purchases.